To Beulah who has faithfully
stood by my side through the
years, inspiring me to keep
Following the Fire

Acknowledgments

I wish to give special acknowedgment to Joanne, my daughter, who has spent many, many hours in careful research, arranging the episodes of my life and making this book very exciting and readable.

I also wish to recognize all my Mennonite brothers and sisters, who have been so forebearing with me. I am grateful that they are seeking all that is theirs in the Holy Spirit. Special thanks to Jamie Buckingham, who lent a helping hand and words of encouragement to help us in the writing of this book. Also, to Barbara Souders, who spent many hours helping me assemble facts from my background.

Contents

Foreword

Following the Fire is a story of a young man with a desire to please God. I have known Gerald Derstine for many years and have had the privilege to share with him and to instruct him in the Scriptures and works of the Holy Spirit. His encounters with people and spiritual forces make this book alive and a special contribution to the Christian church.

The reader should sense the presence of a personal God attempting to break through tradition and obstacles, those blockades that thwart the freedom of the movement of the Holy Spirit. Surely, through reading this book, your life will be encouraged and motivated to pursue in depth a closer relationship with God.

Allow Gerald's life story to add further confirmation of God's deep, intimate desire to communicate with man. I personally recommend this book because I know it will be a supplement to strengthen each reader's Christian faith and commitment.

David J. du Plessis

Introduction

The time had come for Israel to be delivered from Egypt. To realize this purpose, God was looking for a man. Moses was reared by his mother in the royal palace with all the kingly prerogatives. He spent eighty years in the school of academic and pastoral disciplines. But his day finally came. "And the angel of the Lord appeared unto him in a flame of fire" (Exod. 3:2).

Even so, in God's sovereign purpose, He had a plan for Gerald Derstine. Raised in a poor home, with few academic privileges and studies and the physical handicap of stuttering, he was converted, healed, and ordained to the ministry. He and his wife, Beulah, answered God's call to pastor a church in northern Minnesota among the Chippewa Indians. It was in this framework, in the vicissitudes of pastoral work, after praying and fasting for revival, that the "fire of the Lord fell."

Gerald Derstine's story may not be unique. God has called many men and women in wonderful ways. But his story is certainly unusual and significant. It is unusual because God's call is not so spectacular for most of us. It happened during a significant visitation in January, 1955. God was not only speaking to Gerald Derstine; the Lord was calling and speaking to the entire Mennonite church.

Unfortunately, the church was not ready in 1955. It was not until 1972 that official recognition was given to the move of the Spirit in the Mennonite church. I refer to a consultation on the Holy Spirit, a large gathering at Eastern Mennonite College in Harrisonburg, Virginia, that occurred early in 1972. In June of the same year there was a Festival of the Holy Spirit, a large gathering and celebration at Goshen College in Goshen, Indiana. Since then the denomination's interest in charismatic things has spread to the extent that today there are five or six large Mennonite charismatic celebrations in different areas in the U.S.A. and Canada each year.

After the fire fell in Minnesota in 1955, Gerald Derstine had to leave the Mennonite church. A slow but definite reconciliation between him and the denomination is now taking place. Some of the Mennonite leaders associated with Gerald and Beulah in those early years have since gone to be with the Lord. They did not understand what God was doing in His sovereign acts. They tried to be true to their convictions and traditions and the light they had. At least one of them, however, made the long trip from Minnesota to Florida to ask Gerald for forgiveness. Today Gerald and Beulah are invited to many Mennonite churches and communities to witness and to share the realities of God's visitation.

Now Gerald is president of Christian Retreat and Gospel Crusade, Inc. Many good things are taking place at Christian Retreat in Bradenton, Florida, a center that is open every day of the week. Every day except Monday, services are conducted by visiting guest speakers.

Other activities include:

1. A school of ministry where hundreds of young people gather for a ten-week course of Bible Study and ministry.

2. A witness outreach with 150 churches and more than 700 pastors and leaders associated with Gospel Crusade, Inc. in the U.S.A.

3. A foreign missions outreach with missionaries and workers in Haiti, Honduras, the Philippines, Ghana, Israel, South America, Jamaica and by the time this book goes into print, possibly in Europe also.

Where does the money come from? The answer is simple—whom the Lord calls, He sustains. There are many unique things about Gospel Crusade, Inc.

Two things, among many, should be pointed out for all churches to consider. All the followers of Jesus, all professing Christians, need to face seriously these two basic questions.

The first is, "What is the nature of a genuine New Testament spiritual experience?" People are hungering and thirsting to know God in a direct experiential way. The universal charismatic movement and its phenomenal growth is evidence of the unquestionable work of the Holy Spirit. Does the Bible teach what charismatics claim it does? At Christian Retreat, there is a sincere desire and effort to discern the nature of a genuine New Testament spiritual experience according to the Word.

The second question all believers—especially the leaders of churches and denominations—need to consider seriously is: "What is the nature of the unity for which Christ prayed?" Jesus prayed, "That they may all be one" (John 17:21). How can we all be one? What is the nature of that unity? Are we taking Jesus' prayer seriously? How long will we continue to sustain our denominational walls and barriers? At Christian Retreat one experiences a spiritual unity—unity in worship, in fellowship, in purpose. Here one finds Catholics, Episcopalians, Lutherans, Methodists, Presbyterians, Pentecostals, Mennonites and others uniting in praise and worship of their Savior and Lord and seeking to serve Him. This, in part, explains the phenomenal growth of Gospel Crusade. Here one experiences a genuine demonstration of unity.

Following the Fire is the extraordinary story of an ordinary country boy, who with his wife was called by God and is well on the way to a long, happy and fruitful ministry.

Praise the Lord!

Nelson Litwiller, B.A., B.D.
Mennonite bishop & missionary

FOLLOWING THE FIRE

1

"You Will Be Separated"

I took another bite of Beulah's shoofly pie and washed it down with my morning coffee. I stared out the kitchen window. It was cozy and warm in our little house in the Minnesota north woods. Outside, silhouetted against the backdrop of a barely there daylight, the branches of a thousand naked trees, frozen into silence, forked skyward. Snow, deep, billowy, lay like a blanket across the earth, changing every exposed object into a soft lump beneath its thick, white surface. The desolate cry of a timber wolf echoed through the woods, sending snow-shoe rabbits, white mink, and gophers scurrying to safety underground.

I finished the rest of my coffee and set the cup back into the saucer just as a pine tree in the woods behind the house succumbed to the intolerable cold and with a crack like the sound of a shotgun, dug its own grave in the powdery snow. The light of day on the White Earth Indian Reservation ventures forth for only a few short hours in the dead of winter. This morning, the air, so cold it seemed to crystallize, looked like glittery dust as the first rays of sunlight filtered through the trees. A new day had begun.

I pushed back the Bible I had been reading and wondered if Beulah was awake. We hadn't had much sleep these past few days. Excitement like I never dreamed—spiritual excitement—had taken over our house and the little Mennonite church where I was pastor. I had been awake all night, praying, reading the Bible, listening to the Lord.

It was the first week in January, 1955. I'd spent a good part of the summer collecting the ceiling-high stack of firewood in the basement and our faithful little cast-iron furnace was doing its job well. The house wasn't anything fancy. In fact, the bathroom was located eighty feet from the back door through the shoulder-high drifts of snow. But we had an upstairs and heavily insulated walls. It was more than adequate for the extreme temperatures in the woods.

Thus, when the fire of the Holy Spirit began to burn it seemed strangely out of place. I wondered that morning, musing as I took my last sip of coffee, if God always chose strange times and incredible places to reveal himself. Hadn't He chosen a stable for the birth of His Son? Hadn't the announcement of the Messiah been made first to lowly shepherds? Hadn't Jesus chosen an oddball group of men for His disciples? Why should I be so amazed that God had chosen the northern Minnesota woods, on an Indian reservation, in the middle of winter, to start His fire burning in the Mennonite church? Yet, on this sixth day of the most bizarre happenings we had ever witnessed or heard of, I was still dumbfounded and amazed. I didn't pretend to understand it. But by now I was positive God was behind it.

The dull thud of a body crumbling to the floor sent me running into the living room. Amos, the ruggedly handsome eighteen-year-old Amish boy who had come to our home nearly a week before, was lying stiffly on his back in the middle of the floor. By now such an occurrence didn't alarm me. It had been going on for six days already as God seemed to grab people physically, push them down onto the floor, and then speak forth His message through involuntary lips.

Like myself, Amos had been up all night. He had no way of knowing I had been sitting in the kitchen, breathing a silent prayer for direction. Where was all this going? What did God have for me?

"Gerald! Gerald, come here. Take my hand," the young man commanded from his prone position on the hard floor.

I leaned over and grasped his outstretched hand. With eyes closed and body rigid, he began to speak haltingly, yet distinctly:

Gerald, you are going to be separated from the Mennonite church, but do not fear, for I shall give you a greater ministry. I'm going to take you to the outer edges of the Mennonite communities. You shall minister to and teach many of your people the things of my Spirit. Gerald, the Mennonites will not understand now, but they shall later. I am going to send you into the cities— from city to city you shall go, and you shall minister to multitudes and thousands of my people, teaching them about the things of my Spirit.

He let go of my hand and I stared at him. How was he able to know what had been weighing heavily on my mind the past couple days? And how did he know I had just been silently praying, asking questions he had just answered?

Let me think. No, he wasn't even in the room, and besides, I hadn't prayed out loud and hadn't mentioned the prayer to a soul—not even to my wife.

Amos's muscular body was still sprawled out on the floor, but he began to stir now and his eyes opened slowly. A big smile that could only be described as heavenly came across his face. He looked over at me.

"Oh, Gerald," he murmured, "I just had the most beautiful vision of Jesus. Did you see Him?"

"No, I didn't. But you were speaking to me. Didn't you know that? Do you remember what you said?"

He propped himself up on one elbow. "I said something to you?"

My heart started pounding and I walked away as the words he had just spoken rewound and began to play like a tape recorder through my mind. The implications were shocking.

God, I wish you hadn't said that to me. All I ever asked of you was a revival in my little church here among the Indians. I wanted to see more people receive salvation and join the church. That's all. I'm only twenty-six years old and I'm happy being the pastor here. But now you're saying I'll be separated from our people?

The thought weighed like lead in the pit of my stomach. To be a Derstine and not be a Mennonite was highly unlikely. We'd been in the church for hundreds of years. I was sure I was destined to be a Mennonite the rest of my life and I was satisfied with that feeling of certainty.

I looked over at Beulah. She turned from the sink as she wiped the soap from her hands. Her hazel eyes searched mine and asked the same questions I was struggling with. She, too, had a deep-rooted Mennonite heritage and was appropriately attired in the traditional plain, caped dress and small nylon prayer veiling she wore on her head nearly twenty-four hours a day. She had already sacrificed plenty for the young, slightly adventurous missionary-pastor she had married five years before. And she had slowly, but steadily, come to enjoy doing the many little tasks and projects required of her as pastor's wife. She had a lot more gumption than I knew about when I married her. Beulah lowered her eyes now, but not before I caught the quick glance she cast towards the bedroom where our two babies were sleeping.

Even the children were affected by the supernatural happenings that had been taking place the past week. Our one-year-old son, Philip, and three-and-a-half-year-old daughter, Joanne, had not uttered a sound above a whisper the whole time.

Beulah turned back to the dishes, wisely deciding I needed to be left alone with my thoughts at the moment. *You are going to be separated from the Mennonite church. . . .* It didn't make sense. I just knew the church authorities would be thrilled when I told them all the tremendous things God had been doing. They would understand. They knew much more about the Bible than I did and I respected them highly. Yes, I was looking forward to telling them about this.

But then how and why would I be separated from the church? There must be some hidden meaning I wasn't getting.

I am going to send you into the cities . . . to multitudes . . . of my people. That just wasn't possible. The only big city I had ever been to was Philadelphia, and the only people I had spoken to there were drunks and beggars on skid row. Beulah and I used to hand out tracts in the ghettos and witness to the bums and winos who came up to us looking for a handout. They were the only people in a big city I had nerve enough to speak to. They didn't mind that I lacked in confidence and made a few grammatical errors. As long as I bought them a hamburger and coffee they were willing to do anything they were asked, including getting down on their knees and repeating the sinner's prayer.

No, I didn't mind speaking to *them*, but "normal" people, *good* people in their right minds—now they were another story altogether. I just wasn't good enough. I mean I had this inferiority complex that always inhibited me and besides, I hadn't even gone to Bible school.

"Gerald, let's just not worry about it, okay?" Beulah's voice shook me out of my reverie. "If that prophecy really means what it implies I'm sure God will help us through whatever it takes. And no matter what happens, I'm with you anyway. The Lord hasn't let us down yet. He knows that all we want to do is serve Him and if He wants to take us away from the Mennonites, well, He must have a better place for us. Right?"

Her simple logic unnerved me. It seemed reckless. "Sure, it's simple for you to say, but you know that my burden is for *our* people, the Mennonites, not for the whole world! I just don't know where we'd go or how I'd even be able to support you and the children."

"Well, nothing's happened yet and we don't have to worry about it now. And if worse comes to worse, we can find other jobs. We've worked with our hands before and we can do it again." She smiled at me reassuringly, then pulled the plug in the sink, dried her hands on the towel underneath, and disappeared into the bedroom. As far as she was concerned, the subject was closed.

But the fear nagging at my insides wouldn't go away.

But do not fear, for I shall give you a greater ministry. How could I help but fear? Lord, how am I supposed to understand what you mean by a "greater ministry"? Surely you must be talking about the wrong person. You know me—all I've been trained for is running hosiery knitting machines in a factory. You can't expect a whole lot out of someone like me.

I walked over to the overstuffed maroon sofa in the living room, laid down, and closed my eyes. Lord, you're going to have to help me. I want to believe what you said, but this simple human brain finds it hard to figure out.

Gradually a peace settled over me as I drifted to sleep. If I couldn't trust Him now after all I'd seen in the past six days—I never would.

2

Peewee Derstine

Eastern Pennsylvania. Here boroughs, villages, and townships all run together along painfully narrow roads that stretch over hills that look like swells on a heaving ocean. We lived in one of thousands of old townhouses that were exactly alike. My two brothers and I played stickball and kick the can in the alleys behind rows of tiny hedged-in yards. My parents were Mennonites, my grandparents were Mennonites, my great-grandparents were Mennonites, and on back to 1732 when the first Derstine, also a Mennonite, came to America from the east side of the Rhine near Heidelberg, Germany.

The Mennonite faith originated in Europe, founded by a Dutchman named Menno Simons (1496-1561) during the Reformation Movement. He was being educated for the Catholic priesthood when he heard that Swiss Brethren and Anabaptists were being persecuted and killed for their stand for believers' baptism as opposed to infant baptism. These early reformers were being burned at the stake, drowned, beaten, and sold as galley slaves on Italian merchant ships.

Simons made an intensive search of the Scriptures and became convinced he was part of a sinful system. In 1536 he renounced the Catholic church and joined a peaceful group of Anabaptists called Obbenites. The leader of this group, Obbe Phillips, baptized Simons who then received a call to the ministry. He traveled through northern Germany and the Netherlands with a price on his head, preaching and organizing churches. Although many of his followers were martyred for their beliefs, the Mennonite faith was firmly established. In pursuit of religious freedom, believers brought it to the New World in 1663. William Penn, an English Quaker, was instrumental in helping many Mennonites emigrate to America. Most of them, farmers and weavers by trade, settled in Pennsylvania, then eventually pushed westward into Ohio and Indiana and southward into Virginia where large concentrations of Mennonites still exist.

The religion was based on a strong belief in nonresistance. Church members were not allowed to take part in, or support war and violence in any form. As a result, during World War I many Mennonites were sent to detention camps. In later years, however, programs of voluntary alternate service were set up to accommodate their religious convictions. In conjunction with this belief, participation in politics, voting, and the taking of oaths was also prohibited. Although they did not take up arms, the Mennonites were quick to come to the aid of the needs occasioned by war—helping the wounded, homeless and hungry. During the Civil War they took a stand against slavery. Close-knit bonds were formed among themselves and they made it a practice to come to one another's aid in times of tragedy or distress. Jesus' Sermon on the Mount was taken literally and put to practical use. If someone's barn or house burned down, more than enough church members would spend whatever time was necessary to construct a new one. They believed Christians should live in "community."

Life was centered around the church. The buildings themselves were usually unadorned and plain in design. Most were named merely after the town they happened to be in. Pastors and deacons presided over congregations which were divided into districts headed by bishops. Pastors were not salaried by the church so they had to make a living otherwise.

In order to avert pride, the paramount sin, great lengths were taken to resist modern trends and change. Nonconformity to the ways of the world became a standard. Radio and television were forbidden as well as any entertainment outside the church, such as dancing, going to movies, race tracks, or ball games. Drinking and smoking were strictly prohibited and children were given work responsibilities at a young age. Families were large. "Plain clothes" were worn and women were required to wear a head covering at home, in public and in church. Families were tight units. Young people were strongly advised to marry only other Mennonites.

Among their own people, the Pennsylvania Dutch dialect was used and children grew up speaking this mixture of what was commonly described as "Low German and sloppy Dutch," containing a smattering of English. Most of our friends and relatives spoke or at least understood this language that originally came from the Palatinate of Germany. In the early Mennonite churches a modified High German was used. Many people resisted the change to English in subsequent years, although it became evident that the language stymied intellectual progress. Little was printed in the Pennsylvania Dutch dialect and many of the words' similarities to the English caused confusion.

Prayers were said over meals before they were touched

and then thanks was "returned" after meals were completed. In my own home, which was characteristic of most others, these prayers were silent. After about a minute of bowing our heads, I would hear mom or dad take a deep breath, an indication the prayer was over. I never heard my parents pray out loud while I was at home.

"Shunning" those who had strayed from the faith was a chastisement used in the early days, but "only that it be serviceable to one's amendment and not conducive to his ruin." In church, brethren greeted brethren and sisters greeted sisters with the "kiss of charity" (Rom. 16:16). On the other hand, there was the obvious omission of the kiss if one was considered out of fellowship. Foot washing was a regular sacrament as was yearly communion. Water baptism was administered by "pouring" when one joined the church. This consisted of the bishop cupping his hands to receive water poured from a pitcher and then allowing the water to flow over the person's head by sprinkling or pouring.

I was raised in the Mennonite traditions, and to this day I consider myself especially blessed to have been born into a Mennonite family. The Mennonites have a religion based on the highest biblical principles and I am particularly appreciative of their emphasis that Christianity is a way of life, not just something practiced on Sunday mornings. Modern Mennonites have done away with many of the centuries-old traditions, but for many it is only as they are seeking to move on in the things of God.

Mennonite pastors and deacons have been relatively common in the Derstine lineage, although there were more truck drivers, shop owners and farmers in my immediate family. I had no reason to believe I would do other than provide an adequate living for my wife and family one day. I was neither rich, handsome, nor super-intelligent. On the contrary, I always felt it would take considerable doing for me even to fit into the image of middle class and average.

I was born in 1928, the second of three boys. Early in life I learned the necessity of hard work. My teen-aged mother worked as well as my father in order to make ends meet in those depression days.

Durell, my brother who was two years older than I, was my hero and closest friend. I was his shadow. Our earliest escapades evolved under the watchful gaze of an ever-present baby sitter whom we both loathed. She was obese and had body odor and we constantly contrived to escape her territory. I'm sure she earned every penny of her slim wages for what we put her through.

We were always glad when mom came home from work at the clothing factory every afternoon. Although she was a married woman with children, she was still very young and enjoyed playing and teasing with us. Her girlish face had rosy cheeks and twinkling eyes and she smiled a lot. She hated having to go to the hot, stuffy factory away from us all day. But she came from a long line of industrious Dutch ancestors and when working became a necessity she accepted the responsibility matter-of-factly.

Dad drove a bakery truck and I'd tag along with him delivering bread and pastries to our neighbors along the route. Money wasn't easy to come by and as soon as we were old enough, Durell and I would pick wild black-berries and sell them door to door. We certainly didn't get rich, but ten cents a quart seemed a lot in those days!

My parents were strict. The rod was always accessible and was used regularly on the seat of our pants. We feared dad's discipline the most, but mom doled out punishment just as readily. I remember once getting my mouth washed out with soap for telling her a lie.

Every day after our chores, my brothers and I would run out into the alley to join our friends in a lively game of tag or "king of the ash pile." I was always very active and competitive and I learned early that being short required me to compensate in other ways. Along with this I learned another valuable lesson. Never pick on someone bigger than yourself.

One summer day my friends and I were playing in our back yard when the town bully, a husky boy a couple years older than I, approached. He had a reputation for creating trouble wherever he went so I usually tried to stay out of his way. But today I was feeling unusually cocky, especially since I was on my own turf.

I watched him steadily as he got nearer and the minute he glanced in my direction, I stuck out my tongue. I instantly knew I had overstepped my bounds, but it was too late. The next thing I remember was being held aloft by the scruff of the neck and being slung backward like a sack of potatoes. The taste of dirt in my mouth wasn't half as bad as the blow to my ego.

My size wasn't my only handicap. I stuttered. I could barely say my name, much less anything else, without stammering profusely. I always wished I'd had a different name since G's and D's were the hardest letters for me to pronounce. I dreaded having to answer the phone and only did so when there was no one else in the house. I knew the caller would always ask who had answered, so when the phone started ringing, I would begin saying my name before I picked up the receiver.

"G-G-G-G-GERALD D-D-D-D-D-D-DERSTINE!!" I'd explode into the receiver as I picked it up.

Of course, my voice was usually so loud and distorted that they'd ask, "Who did you say this was?" And I'd have to go through the whole frustrating process again.

I grew painfully shy. Some of my classmates in school taunted and made fun of me and I learned to make friends only with those I felt were inferior like I was. I could never answer questions out loud in class and sometimes I felt I would burst inside at not being able to join in a lively conversation.

There was one way in which I could really express myself. That was through music. Although musical instruments were forbidden in the Mennonite church then, we had a piano in our home and dad played it regularly. I learned how to harmonize in church where the entire congregation would sing in four-part harmony. The men and boys all sat on one side singing tenor and bass, and the women and girls were across the aisle singing soprano and alto. To an outsider, the congregation sounded like a choir! I was an adult before I discovered that many people could not sing any one of four parts by ear.

Many years later when I was ministering in Indonesia I panicked when one of the Chinese pastors asked if I would sing a solo.

"Oh, no," I said, shaking my head emphatically. "I play the accordion and piano and organ, but I'm not a soloist."

"But you are from America, and all Americans can sing. Please, you sing solo." He was persistent.

"No, I couldn't sing," I laughed nervously. This little guy wasn't going to let me off the hook. "I do sing with my wife sometimes, and our family sings together, but I have never sung a solo."

The smile never left his face and I couldn't see his eyes because they were so squinched up. His head bobbed up and down like he hadn't even heard what I said.

"Please, Brudder Derstine, you sing tonight."

All of a sudden the words from one of my own sermons ran like a news flash before my eyes. "Never say 'no' when you're asked to do something for the glory of God. Even if you think you can't do it, or if you've never done it before, do it anyway! You can't get any worse than what you are now. You can only improve...."

"Okay," I said resignedly. "I'll sing tonight." It would be his embarrassment, I analyzed, if I made a flop. Not mine. I tried to tell him I couldn't sing, but he didn't accept it. On the other hand, there was the remote chance that I *was* a soloist. I'd never tried it, so how did I know for sure?

I sang that night, providing my own accordion accompaniment. And to my utter amazement the people seemed to like it. They didn't boo me off the stage or even politely tell me never to sing again. In fact, the pastor asked me to sing again the next night. And the next.

As it turned out, for the next few weeks as I traveled to different cities and ministered to thousands of people all over Java, I was asked to sing a solo everywhere I went. I became known as the "singing American evangelist" in the country of Indonesia.

In one city, a group of teen-agers came giggling up to me after the service. One of them stepped up to me shyly and asked, "'Are you Pat Boone's papa?" I chose to take it as a compliment. Pat was the rage in their country at that time and they must have imagined some sort of resemblance. I was flattered to be compared in any way with Pat, although I certainly would have been happier if they had asked if I was his brother.

By the time I left Indonesia I was actually enjoying singing solos. I still don't consider myself a soloist by any means—unless I'm in Indonesia. Through that experience I learned an important truth about God's enabling power, however.

Church to the Derstines was not just a weekly ritual, but a daily way of life. Dad had his family lined up in a pew every time the church doors opened. We weren't deposited in a nursery in the back to be picked up after the service either. We were ordered to sit quietly in the sanctuary throughout the service. Sometimes this seemed to be next to impossible. Dad would pinch us hard once or twice and when that didn't work he'd grab us firmly, march us down the aisle, out behind the building, and we'd have a painful, but effective, "laying on of hands." Although no one needed the old horse barn behind the church any longer, I think they left it standing for the convenience of fathers like mine.

"Gerald! Durell! Hurry up! We'll be late yet," mom was calling in her thick Dutch accent as she fed little Willie his breakfast. She and dad used to talk to each other in Pennsylvania Dutch when they wanted to keep a secret from us boys, but after a while we picked up the dialect ourselves and they had to resort to other methods. I was nine years old and this Sunday morning was typically frantic as mom tried to get us ready for Sunday school.

As we entered the sanctuary, mom left us boys with

dad and went across the aisle to sit with the women. It was quiet except for the shuffling of peoples' feet and the rustling of clothing as people slid into the plain wooden pews. I settled in beside dad and my eyes scanned the chairs behind the pulpit.

All at once I sat up straight. There was my Uncle Llewelyn Groff. He was a missionary to the Chippewa Indians up in the north woods of Minnesota and happened to be my favorite minister. Visions of Indian teepees with bows and and arrows poking from the flaps danced through my head. Just think! To be able to live on an Indian reservation way back in the woods—

The reedy sound of the song leader's pitch pipe invaded my daydream. I pulled a hymn book out of the rack in front of me, peeked over Durell's shoulder to find the page, and then raised my still-soprano voice along with the men's tenor and bass. Although the singing part of the service was always my favorite, it seemed unusually long this morning.

Finally, the hymn books rattled back into their racks and Uncle Llewelyn was introduced. I was proud he was my uncle. He wore the traditional plain-cut Mennonite suit as did all the men who were members of the church. The coat was always in a solid dark color, buttoned up to the neck, with no tie. We could always tell at first glance whether a person was a Christian by the clothes he wore.

"Please turn in your Bibles to Matthew 28:19. 'Go ye therefore, and teach all nations, baptizing them in the name of the Father, and of the Son, and of the Holy Ghost.' " He opened with that familiar passage, the Great Commission, then proceeded to give experiences he and his family had encountered among the Indians. I was a mite disappointed to learn they lived in a travel trailer instead of a teepee, but then decided that must be almost as exciting—like camping out all the time.

"The Lord called us to work among the Chippewa people," he was saying, "and we want to tell them about God, bring them into the church, and help them make a better life for themselves."

As he talked, I began to feel more than just my initial excitement over his adventures. It was something else— a disturbing something that made my heart beat fast. I heard no voices, but I knew, I just *knew* that one day I would be a missionary. Beyond a shadow of doubt I knew.

The service was dismissed, and disengaging my hand from dad's, I ran to look for my two buddies.

"Johnny! Herman! D-d-did you listen to w-what Uncle L-lewelyn said? D-d-didn't that s-sound neat?" I stammered.

"Yeah, it sounded exciting all right," Johnny answered. "Boy, I sure wish I could go to an Indian reservation."

"Me too," Herman added.

An idea popped into my head. "Hey, I know w-what we can d-do. Why don't we s-s-start saving our money so w-when we grow up we c-can go to M-M-Minnesota?"

"Yeah, that would be neat!" they chorused together. "Let's do it. We ought to have a bundle by the time we're sixteen!"

"Okay, n-now look," I said. "Here's what we can do. Every S-sunday w-when we come to Sunday s-school, we can p-put the money we've saved into a j-j-jar. With th-three of us like this, our s-savings will grow m-much faster. J-just think what we could s-save in one year!"

Herman and Johnny nodded in agreement, and our pact was sealed. None of us found it easy to come by the pennies, nickles, and dimes we contributed to our little fund each Sunday. But we found that by denying ourselves the occasional candy bars, ice cream cones, and bubble gum we'd normally manage to get through the week, we were able to drop some coins into the jar. I would regularly scout the neighborhood gutters and trash cans for pop bottles. Every time I was tempted to spend my nickels on candy, I'd remember the little jar and slip the coins back into my pocket. But then on Sunday morning when I could add to the growing stack of change, it was worth it and I would feel happy inside.

It took about nine months for the novelty to wear off. First Johnny became discouraged and stopped contributing to the jar. That really disappointed me. Herman continued awhile longer before he lost interest and backed out. I was crushed. Our little project wasn't going to work and we would have to cancel our trip. As I contemplated the situation, I decided it really wasn't as exciting as it had first seemed. And it surely wasn't any fun continuing on by myself. So that spelled the end of my ambitions of being a missionary to the Indians. Or so I thought.

3

My Accordion and All That Jazz

As I entered my teens, church and all it represented bored me. Dad and mom made me attend, but aside from giving me a chance to pal around with my friends and relatives, it was something to be endured. I wasn't the only one who felt that way. In fact, I became accustomed to seeing the older men nod off to sleep during most of the services. I figured I wouldn't have to worry about getting serious about religion until I was closer to dying. In the meantime I was going to have some fun.

In spite of my stammering condition, I became quite popular in high school. "Peewee" Derstine first gained recognition as a champion marble shooter. I developed skill playing marbles and had the biggest and best collection in the school. My special "shooter" was envied and respected by many. I even received a special certificate and invitation to the state competition, but my joy over this was short-lived when my folks forbade me to enter. Our religion did not approve of such frivolities.

Dad was, however, a little more progressive than some of our friends and he allowed me to take part in school sports. In the tenth grade, believe it or not, I was appointed captain of the basketball team—all five feet six inches of me! What I lacked in height, I made up for in speed. I could dribble that ball around the court and through those long legs faster than anybody. Our team wasn't anything to brag about that year, but the experience helped to boost my self-confidence just a little bit more.

Along with my studies and sports activities I even managed to slip in a part-time job. I worked my first "real" job at Martin's Dairy for thirty-five cents an hour cleaning floors and helping out with the chores.

That same year, I managed to save enough money to buy myself an accordion. Music was in my blood and I spent hours listening to Dick Cantino on the radio. I knew I could play like him if I only had the chance. So when I came home with my brand new instrument I was ready to become a star. I'd practice by the hour until mom would put her hands over her ears and shoo me out the door. I suppose she wouldn't have minded so much if I'd been boning up on "Amazing Grace" or "Sweet Hour of Prayer," but my preferences were along the lines of "Sentimental Journey" and "Chattanooga Choo-choo."

Before long, word got out that I could play a mean tune on the accordion. I was asked to play for parties and dances and if I could have gotten away with it I would have made the rounds. Playing my accordion helped mask for a few moments my still-present shyness and feelings of inferiority. Somehow when I was the center of attention, with that squeeze box cradled between my arms and a big smile on my face, I felt accepted. They liked me, and the feeling was intoxicating.

Little by little I drifted away from the church. I came to resent all the restrictions imposed upon me as a Mennonite. Anything fun was bad. Dancing was a sin, and school proms were positively out of the question.

Movie theaters, bowling alleys, pool halls, and non-Mennonite girls were also forbidden. In fact, most any activity that was not sponsored by the church was frowned on. I felt cheated and I strained against the rules that were supposed to keep me on the straight and narrow.

When one of my buddies, Charlie, sauntered over to me one day and started talking about the carnival that had just come to town I didn't pay much attention. I would never be permitted to go. But then he said something that made me sit up and listen.

"Hey, Gerry, did you know they're having an amateur talent contest over at the carnival?"

"Yeah, so what?" I countered.

"Well, man, you know some of us guys were talking and we thought you should show 'em how you can play that accordion. You really are pretty good, you know. I bet you could win."

My mind started racing. "Aw—I don't know—"

"Oh, come on. You could do it. They're even giving out cash prizes!"

I knew I could do it, and the thought excited me. Lord knows I could use the money, I reasoned. But there was only one catch. Or rather there were two—dad and mom. There was *no* way they'd allow me to do something like that. *No way.* But this could be my big break!

The more I mulled it over, the more I knew I was going to be in that contest. All the guys wanted me to do it and I couldn't let them down. Besides, I rationalized, I wouldn't really be doing anything wrong.

I determined not to tell my folks. What they didn't know wouldn't hurt them.

As I walked up onto the stage that night, my excitement overwhelmed the knot of guilt in my stomach. My eyes scanned the crowd gathered in the open air. Good. The only familiar faces I saw were my school friends.

When the applause died, I began to squeeze out the strains of the "Repasz Band March." I decided that by keeping my eyes glued to the keyboard the butterflies fluttering around inside would stay a little calmer. This had to be good. I'd practiced it a hundred times.

I hit the final chord and looked up and smiled. I'd done it! And from the way the crowd was clapping I knew I'd been a hit.

By the end of the evening, the competition had been narrowed down to an eight-year-old boy with a disgustingly angelic voice—and me. I had to repeat my performance two more times before the judges finally awarded the first prize to the boy soloist. I received second prize— a crisp ten-dollar bill.

Even at that I was elated. My friends wouldn't stop slapping me on the back and pumping my hand.

"We knew you could do it, Gerry!" they exclaimed.

"Yeah, you were really good. We were all rootin' for you! You should have gotten first prize, though. You were lots better than that little kid."

I drank in the praise. This had to be the best day of my life. The hard little knot in my stomach had almost disappeared. Mom and dad would never be the wiser. Besides, I was beginning to find out the world was a lot more exciting than the closely protected one I had grown up in.

My elation was not to last. My accomplishment happened to be reported in the local paper and although my dad was not a subscriber someone at work pointed out my name to him. I was awarded a sound scolding and several restrictions.

When Durell bought his first car we both took full advantage of our freedom. We were going to find out for ourselves why certain things were so strictly forbidden. We made the rounds of all the taboo places—movie theaters, pool halls, bowling alleys. I especially liked to play pool although my first choice was always listening to a good jazz band.

It was no fun being at home anyway. Mom was constantly on our backs about something. It seemed we never did anything right—never pleased her. If there was a flaw to be found in us, or in anyone else for that matter, she pointed it out. It wasn't until years later after having children of my own and discovering the same parental traits in myself that I was willing to understand and forgive her. I discovered that there's no danger of a child becoming spoiled if discipline, strict as it may be, is proportionately balanced with sincere and consistent encouragement and every effort to build his own self-worth. The sin of pride is very different than the development of a healthy self-confidence. Only the Holy Spirit is able to break the patterns of behavior that are passed down from generation to generation. And my mom turned out to be a beautiful example of this.

My character went from bad to worse. Sneaking out of the house by way of my weak excuses became easier. I did everything I could to be like all the other kids in school. My religion embarrassed me. I was still too shy to be very aggressive with girls, but my best friend was tall, handsome, and very popular and he would take me under his wing. He'd fix me up with a date and we'd hit the town.

Yet I could never fully enjoy the freedoms I was taking. I was conscientious enough to care what mom and dad thought and along with being plagued by guilt feelings

I was always nagged by a fear of being found out. Furthermore, they usually did manage to find out what I was up to and lately had been threatening to pull me out of public school and send me to a Mennonite parochial school in Virginia. I had graduated from tenth grade as salutatorian of my class and certainly didn't want to change schools and friends at that point. I cringed at the thought of going to a church school.

But one day mom approached me with, "Gerald, you're becoming too wild. You're getting too much out of hand for us and we've decided you *must* go to Eastern Mennonite High School. It's all settled and I've sent for the applications, so don't argue."

Well, I argued all right. They just couldn't do this to me! But I had no alternative. It was either go there or quit school altogether, and I certainly wanted to get my high school diploma. Mom did promise, though, that I could come back and complete my last year at the local high school if I still wanted to. She had hopes that after spending my junior year at EMHS in Harrisonburg, Virginia, I'd come to enjoy it and would want to stay. But I was certain I would hate it.

I was right. I hated it. And I made every effort to demonstrate the fact. I hadn't gone of my own free will and I wasn't giving anyone the satisfaction of thinking they were going to reform me.

An incident that had occurred a few months earlier as I was filling out my application still bugged me. In fact it disturbed me a lot more than I was willing to admit, even to myself.

When my application forms came in the mail, I sat down and grudgingly filled in all the blanks. Mom picked up the completed form and scanned it. She stopped abruptly and looked at me.

"Gerald, why did you answer yes to this question?"

"What question?" I asked.

"Why, the one that asks if you're a Christian," she answered, pointing to the paper.

I stared at her. "Well, b-b-because I *am* a Christian!"

"No, you're not," she said. "You've never joined the church and been baptized. You're not a Christian. You'll have to be honest and change your answer."

My face grew hot. "How can you say I'm n-not a C-Christian? Y-you don't know. Just b-because I haven't joined the ch-church doesn't mean I'm a s-sinner. Huh! Anyway, I'm n-not so sure I even want to b-become a M-Mennonite, so there!"

As the realization sank in that mom really meant what she said, I began to fidget. How could she say that? Here I'd been going to church since I was born and now she was saying I wasn't even a Christian.

I tried to shrug it off. Oh, well, if in fact I wasn't a Christian, I wasn't so sure I wanted to become one. Most of the ones I had seen really didn't impress me that much and besides, I was going to get the most out of life. Being a Christian was boring. I could save it till I got old like her. Then I could worry about getting to heaven.

Mom watched over my shoulder as I scratched out my yes and printed no.

Except for one other student, I was the only "non-Christian" in my class. I'm sure everyone was aware of that fact. For this reason my rebellion was tolerated perhaps a little more than that of my Mennonite classmates.

The highlight of each school year at EMHS was a two-week revival at which our daily attendance was mandatory. I particularly dreaded the approach of this series of meetings and finally decided to skip the whole event. I knew the services would be complete with altar call and invitation for salvation and I didn't like the uncomfortable feelings I experienced during such intense moments.

So after some careful planning I fixed up a little hide-out in the closet of my dorm room. It was complete with plenty of sports magazines, comic books, and potato chips. One light bulb dangled from the ceiling and after stuffing all the cracks around the door with towels, I felt pretty secure.

Each evening after all the boys were supposed to have gone to the meeting, the dean made his rounds of all the rooms just to double-check. He'd never look in the closet, though. When the service was over, my roommate would come in, knock on the door, and let me know the coast was clear.

It worked fine for a while. My ingenuity surprised even me. But then the inevitable happened.

I was sitting in my little nest, cozily reading about the latest dragsters when my light suddenly went out. That crazy roomie must be playing tricks on me, I thought. Meeting must have let out early.

"Hey, w-what's goin' on? T-turn that light back on!" I yelled.

Suddenly the door swung open and I stood face to face with the dean. My breath caught in my throat.

"Oh, it's y-y-you," I mumbled lamely. My mind raced. There was only one way I was going to get out of this one. And I had to do it fast.

"Say, uh, I've b-been th-thinking, and uh, I think I'm r-ready to j-join the church. Yeah, I've been d-doing some real s-serious 'considerating.' When d-do you think they'll be b-baptizing new members?" I concentrated on making my face as innocent and serious as possible.

He fell for it. He'd been wanting to hear those words for a long time. And as much as I hated it there, I couldn't bear the thought of being sent home and having to face mom and dad.

I ended up with a stern reprimand and membership in the Mennonite church. A stiff price, I decided, but it could have been worse. I determined to try my best to shape up. Outwardly, anyway, if not inwardly.

The one thing I refused to leave behind upon coming to parochial school was my accordion. Musical instruments, along with radios, were strictly forbidden in the school in those days. I just couldn't conceive, though, of going through the entire year not being able to pick up my squeeze box, so I brought it along.

Probably figuring I was better off playing my accordion than getting myself into more serious trouble, the school authorities gave me permission. However, it carried a certain restriction; my music had to be played out of earshot of the campus.

That didn't discourage me. In fact, I kind of enjoyed traipsing up the grassy hill out behind the school. I had to play a little louder to hear myself out in the open air, and I did manage to attract an audience once in a while, but it also helped to keep my mind occupied.

Unfortunately, joining the church didn't produce the effect in me that dad and mom had expected. I didn't change my mind about finishing my senior year at Lansdale High. I came home from EMHS as rebellious as ever, looking forward to getting back with my old friends.

During that next year I was able to save enough of my

hard-earned dollars to make a down payment on my very first car—a slick 1937 Pontiac coupe. Was I ever proud of that beauty! She had a glistening black body accented by crimson pinstripes along her sides, and I pampered her inside and out. Nothing quite compared to the sensation of twisting the key in the ignition and hearing that V-8 jump to life. And it definitely had an instant effect on my popularity with the women!

I double-dated quite often with my best friend, Bob, and his date. He came from a prominent family and being especially good-looking and charming, he had no trouble dating whomever he pleased.

Although I was still shy, I was learning to cope with my inferiority complex. My stuttering was an embarrassing handicap, especially when it came to asking for a date, yet I refused to let it control my life. I determined that even if I would always be a stammerer, I would still make something of myself. This optimistic and positive attitude was probably what won me so many friends in high school and those closest to me had all but forgotten about my handicap.

I'll never forget what happened with one of the first girls I dated. I had taken her out a few times and we'd always had fun, but I soon realized she really wasn't my type. She was a Mennonite girl and nice looking, but she came on too strong. I didn't like that in a girl. I knew she was making more out of our relationship than there was and I had to put a stop to it.

So as we stood on her darkened porch one night I decided to break the news gently. We'd had a good time that night and the moon was shining and the whole atmosphere of the moment was contradictory to what I knew I had to say.

"L-listen, I'll just c-call you and l-let you know about g-going out again," I said. "I'm pretty busy r-right now and well, l-let's just not t-tie each other down. Okay?" She got the message all right. Before I knew what was happening she'd fainted! I chalked it down later as my first exposure to man's age-old bewilderment of the female species.

4

Beulah

It was the summer of 1947. The days were typically long, hot, and muggy, and I looked forward to seeing the leaves on the big maple in front of the house begin to lose some of their greenness. My high school diploma was freshly hung on the bedroom wall. I was the proud owner of a snappy little piece of transportation, and I had a good job down at the hosiery mill. Being a free and independent citizen was going to be very nice.

I smiled as I remembered the little line written next to my yearbook picture. It was supposed to predict the profession in life each student was most apt to attain. Mine read: "Gerald Derstine—successful bellhop of a large hotel." Well, right now I was satisfied to be a hosiery knitter.

But this was an especially fine day since I just happened to be on my way to ask a pretty little lady out for a date. Boy, would she be surprised! Oh, she was used to seeing me around. I had been dating her best friend for the past six months, and she had been dating my best friend, so we'd double-dated quite often. But both of us, for one reason or another, had just broken up with our steadies.

It was funny. I'd never thought twice about asking Beulah Hackman out before. I guess it was because she and her boyfriend seemed pretty permanent. They made a handsome couple and she was always so outgoing and spontaneous. There were lots of laughs when the four of us went out together. Beulah was one of those girls fortunate enough to have acquired a car by the time she was sixteen. In fact, she was fondly known in our young circle as "Cowboy Beulah"—for her famous "lead foot."

For the past few weeks I'd begun to think seriously of the future—my own in particular. I hadn't really contemplated marriage before, but I knew that one day I'd want to settle down. I also knew that the girl I had been dating wasn't the one for me. She was a career-minded type and that wasn't what I wanted in a wife. I preferred someone who'd have a good home-cooked meal waiting on the table when I got home from work.

It seemed natural for me to start thinking about Beulah. And the more I thought about her, the more excited I became.

Now I'd gotten up my nerve. I had to ask her out. I tried to stifle the thought that she might turn me down. For some reason I didn't think she would.

The old brick townhouse duplex she shared with her mother was just a short way from ours. Beulah was the youngest of ten children and her father had died when she was only six years old. She had had to drop out of school after the eighth grade in order to help her mother make ends meet. They both worked at one of the textile factories. Beulah ran a sewing machine, making men's shirts. I admired her tenacity.

As I pulled up to the curb in front of her house, I noticed she was already out on the front porch. Perfect! She glanced up at me and smiled when she saw who I was. Her face was flushed from the heat and her wavy golden hair glinted in the sun.

"Well, hi, Gerald!" she exclaimed. "Haven't seen you for a while." She wiped her hands on her stained apron. "You'll have to excuse the way I look. I've been helping mom can peaches all afternoon."

"Oh, th-that's okay. You l-look fine to me." Well, I thought, here goes.

"S-say, uh, I thought may-maybe you'd like to go out with m-me tomorrow night. We c-could go to a m-movie or something."

There was just an instant of hesitation before she said, "Why sure, I guess I could. Yeah, that would be fun. I'm kinda tired of sitting around anyway."

"Great! About s-six then?"

"Fine with me, Gerald. See you then!"

Wow. That was easy enough. I smiled at her and turned to go back to my car. All at once I felt a stabbing pain in my gut. Nerves, that's all it is, I thought. But it got worse and I almost doubled over as I pressed my hands over the pain. Maybe it was a severe case of indigestion. I tried to remember what I had eaten for lunch. Man, this was embarrassing, but I wasn't going to be able to take it much longer. I glanced over my shoulder and saw Beulah staring at me strangely.

"Are you okay?" she called.

"Oh, sure, I'm fine," I said, trying to straighten up and act normally. Just gotta make it to the car and I'll be all right. I eased onto the seat and pulled away from the curb.

When I got home mom immediately insisted I go to bed. She tried all her home remedies on me and when they didn't work, she finally rushed me to the hospital. By that time I was in sheer agony.

It wasn't long before I found myself on the operating table. Diagnosis: acute appendicitis. What rotten luck, I fumed. My first date with Beulah and here I was in a hospital bed. It just couldn't be.

When I woke up a few hours later I noticed I was sharing my room with another guy. He glanced over at me and grinned.

"Hi ya'! My name's Hackman. What's yours?"

My ears perked up. Hackman? That is Beulah's last name.

"I'm Gerald Derstine," I answered. "Did you say 'Hackman'? Do you know Beulah Hackman?"

"Sure, she's my cousin. She'll probably drop by here. Why? You know her?"

"Uh-huh. Yeah, I do." What a stroke of luck!

Beulah and I shared our first date there in the hospital, with me flat on my back and she sitting on a chair close to my bed. Not the most romantic of dates, but it did wonders for my speedy recovery!

Our courtship lasted for the next two years. The more I got to know this girl, the more I liked her. She had been born and raised a Mennonite, but she also had the same streak of rebellion that I contended with. She wasn't satisfied with the church. She didn't wear the little traditional prayer veiling all the time or the plain, solemn clothing. I admired her independence and carefree ways.

It wasn't long before I grew to love this sweet, happy-faced girl. I found hidden beneath that uninhibited exterior a gentle, thoughtful, and caring woman. Innately sensitive to the needs of others to the exclusion of her own needs, she was mature beyond her years. I wanted her to spend the rest of her life with me.

When I finally proposed to her, I asked another

question at the same time that seemed ludicrous even to me. But for some reason it came out.

"Beulah, before you make up your mind for sure that you really want to marry me, I have to ask you something else. W-would you still want to m-marry me if I were to be a preacher or m-minister someday? I mean, w-would you b-be willing to s-spend your life as a p-preacher's wife?"

She looked startled and a little perplexed. In fact, I myself didn't know why I'd said something like that. Looking back on it later it may have had something to do with a dream I'd been having with disturbing frequency. In that dream I was preaching—not only to a congregation of white, American faces, but to black and Oriental faces. It was nonsensical for me to have dreams like that, especially since I knew I wasn't even living a Christian life.

Beulah knit her brow and looked at me intently. "Yes, Gerald, it would be all right," she answered slowly. "As long as we're together, whatever you feel you have to do will be okay with me. I'm not afraid of anything."

At this stage of being in love it's so easy to make concessions and promises and we were no less starry-eyed than anyone else at that point.

I breathed a sigh of relief as I took her in my arms. Yes, she was the one all right. I was sure of it now.

We had a traditional Mennonite wedding on June 25, 1949. Beulah got special permission to wear white pumps instead of the accepted black shoes and we were given the privilege of having an octet of singers provide the musical background, a cappella of course. I had requested a quartet, but was turned down on the premise that it would be too worldly. The church authorities finally consented to an octet on the condition that they would sing from the back of the church. Normally, the only music in a wedding would be congregational singing. There would be no rings exchanged.

My bride was beautiful. Her trim, petite figure enhanced the simple elegance of her white calf-length dress. Her face was radiant and the twinkle in her eye caught and held my own as we stood side by side in front of the altar.

"And now I pronounce you man and wife: Mr. and Mrs. Gerald Derstine." At last! She was all mine. Forever.

If only she could have known what lay ahead. If only I could have known. Thank God, He did not reveal it to us. Yet.

5

Saved, and Healed of Stuttering

I talked my new bride into sharing my childhood fantasy and we drove out to the Minnesota north woods to visit my uncle, the missionary. It was during our ten-day honeymoon on the White Earth Indian Reservation that I ran into someone who started the wheels turning in my spiritually dormant mind. A Mennonite Bible teacher told me of an evangelist named William Branham whom he had just seen and heard in Detroit.

"Gerald, what was so exciting about this man was that he actually healed people from sicknesses," he exclaimed. "People who came in wheelchairs just got up and walked, and blind people began to see—"

"Hey, w-wait a minute," I interrupted, "you d-don't really b-believe that was f-for real, do you?"

"Well, it sure looked real to me. I saw it with my own two eyes. The preacher would pray, then call out some disease, point to someone, and they'd stand up. Next thing you knew they'd be running around or jumping up and down or something. It really was something I wouldn't have believed if I hadn't seen it with my own eyes. And there were literally thousands of people there."

"Huh," I mused. "That does sound interesting. I d-don't know, though. I'd b-be careful about going t-to things like that if I were you. N-no telling what could happen."

But my curiosity was undeniably piqued. I had to see this. People actually getting healed by God? Was it truly possible? I knew that people got healed in the Bible—I had learned that in Sunday school. But my teachers always implied it only happened back then. There was no such thing as "divine healing" today. But if there indeed *was*—

I hardly dared allow myself to think of the possibility of my own healing. I had already sent off for some mail-order course that was supposed to cure stammerers. It cost $300 and although they gave no ironclad guarantees, there was always a chance it would work.

All the way back home to Pennsylvania I pondered what I'd heard. Could there really be something more to religion than what I'd seen? For all my unbelief there was still a spark that compelled me to keep searching. It was frustrating. God, I thought, why can't I just forget about you and live my own life?

On the other hand, I'd kind of like to see what this guy's talking about. Just out of curiosity's sake. See it for myself. Wouldn't hurt anything to see it just once.

I got my chance a couple months later. Beulah and I were just beginning to find out what married life was about. I was already willing to admit it wasn't all I thought it would be, and worse than that I had the feeling I was to blame. I'd come home from work tired and frustrated and it turned out Beulah wasn't as sweet and perfect as I thought she was. Any little thing would set me off and the "old German" in me would lash out at her. She'd cried herself to sleep more than once. Life wasn't nearly as fulfilling as I thought it should be. Worse than that, it was very boring.

So when dad mentioned that some faith healers, T.L. Osborn and Gordon Lindsay, were coming to town I determined to go and see for myself if the things my friend had said were true.

I wasn't quiet prepared for what I saw as Beulah and I drove into the huge grassy parking lot of the tent revival meeting. Cars and people covered the place. Masses of them. I was glad we'd arrived a little early. There were already thousands of people under the tent, filling the chairs and then standing all around the back. Where did they all come from? And why were they all there? There was such an air of excitement—I almost felt guilty being there. Kind of like the time I'd sneaked to the carnival.

As we ducked under the flap to stand behind the back chairs the smell of sawdust and canvas greeted our nostrils. The sight that caught my eyes first was the collection of paraphernalia strung out in long lines from the top of the tent. There were metal wheelchairs of all sizes, leg and back braces of innumerable shapes, and hundreds of canes and crutches. I was spellbound.

The crowd hushed suddenly as a man came to the podium. His voice boomed through the huge, bell-shaped loudspeakers.

"Let's all stand together and sing, 'O, How I Love Jesus.'" The organ swelled as five thousand voices sang out the familiar tune. It was awesome. I'd never heard anything that sounded so beautiful. I looked around at the faces and saw a happiness and anticipation I couldn't comprehend. They sang song after song, all of them about love and Jesus. Some of them I'd heard before and some were foreign to me, but they were all sung with a fervency I had never seen in church before.

It wasn't long before I found myself responding to that

contagious atmosphere. Inside, anyway. Oh, I wished I could be that free. I sat there willing myself not to show any emotion, but what I was feeling inside was almost forcing the tears to my eyes. I wished I could be as free and uninhibited as these people were. They even clapped their hands to some of the songs and when they prayed they would raise their hands in the air. And they seemed to enjoy it.

Later on when I began to see with my own eyes the miraculous healings of so many people who were obviously sick and deformed, I was forced to believe. I knew what we were witnessing was something that wasn't taught in our church, yet here I was seeing it.

Greater than what I saw was what I felt. A warm, happy sensation followed us home and lingered for days.

We went back time after time. Mom and dad were getting worried about us. They'd heard strange reports about those healing campaigns. I finally convinced them to come along with us one night. Mom tucked her Bible in her purse and determined to follow every Scripture in order to prove to us where they were in error. She figured then we would see the dangers we were exposing ourselves to.

But by the end of the evening, she was no farther than when she had started. Everything the preacher said checked out with her Bible. The only thing she ended up with was that he was wearing a necktie and a gold wedding band on his finger—worldly accessories that only a proud, haughty person would wear. And the preacher's wife wore a necklace and even had bobbed hair! Surely they couldn't be Christians, or at least very good Christians, looking like that.

Mom and dad didn't bother us after that though. And it

wasn't until the fifth time we went and stood around the back of the tent that we broke.

The message had been preached and an invitation for salvation was being given. I felt like crying.

"Anyone who wants to give his life to the Lord tonight just raise your hand. If you want the Lord Jesus to forgive you and take away all that guilt and unhappiness, give yourself to Him tonight," the preacher entreated, as the organ played softly in the background.

I felt Beulah's hand slip into mine and when I glanced at her and saw the tears glistening in her eyes I knew she was feeling the same thing I was. People around us were lifting their arms in that air as they responded to the call. I yearned to give in to that "something" that urged me to do the same. But my arms felt as if they were weighted down with lead. They wouldn't budge.

"Come. Slip up your hand, then stand up and come down the aisle to the front where I can pray for you."

I recoiled at the thought of having to walk down front and maybe having to talk to somebody. I couldn't even get my hand up.

Yet I was ready to burst inside. There was no question as to what I wanted. With my head bowed, I quietly asked Jesus Christ to come into my heart. At that moment I wanted Him more than anything else in this world.

As soon as I uttered that silent prayer, I was free. A peace like I had never felt before enveloped me and I knew I was a child of God. For the first time in my life I really *knew*. It was as simple as that. And I hadn't even raised my hand.

Just then Beulah squeezed my hand and I knew she had done the same thing I had. She was sniffling and dabbing at her eyes with a Kleenex.

We were finally one.

I guess the first indication of my conversion was an insatiable desire to read the Bible. I'd read it for hours on end. One chapter after the other, one book after the next. I just couldn't get enough. I'd take my Bible to the factory and memorize verses while my machine ran. In fact, I read my Bible so much that mom and dad noticed what I was doing and began to worry about me.

"Gerald, you shouldn't read so much at one time. It's just not normal."

"W-why not, mom?"

"Well, you just shouldn't get so serious about it. I'm not saying you shouldn't read the Bible—just don't do it so much. I mean you could lose your mind if you keep up what you're doing. I don't want you ending up in some mental institution."

"Aw, mom, you just don't understand," I said, shaking my head.

We started having Friday night Bible studies in our home. Several of our young married friends would come over and we'd search the Scriptures. Sometimes we'd play a tape of a Mennonite evangelist who was popular in those days, George Brunk. Other times we'd invite someone to speak to us.

The thing that particularly excited me as I read through the Bible were the many references to healing that I'd never known were there before. Divine, miraculous healings. After I was saved at the Osborn meeting I determined in my heart to claim my own healing. T.L. Osborn had said that if you claimed the promises in the Bible and then confessed with your mouth what you believed, you would be healed. It sounded simple.

So I started quoting verses like 1 Peter 2:24, "By whose

stripes ye were healed," and Matthew 8:17, He "Himself took our infirmities, and bare our sicknesses. . . ." I quoted them to myself and to anyone who would listen. I stuttered as I told my friends that "by His stripes I am already healed." Then I'd stammer my verses to them. Needless to say, my friends began looking at me a little strangely. Actually, after a while I think they began to feel sorry for me.

"B-by His stripes I am h-h-healed. The B-Bible promises m-me that. You know, o-o-one of these days I'm g-gonna be talking j-just like everybody else. I j-j-just know it!"

And I *did* know it. I also knew I'd go on saying that the rest of my life—even if I never saw the results. At least I knew I'd be perfectly well in heaven.

My friends would just smile indulgently and pat me on the back. Then they would try to change the subject. They had known me a long time and picturing me without my speech impediment was unimaginable. My family was embarrassed. Mom would say, "Gerald, I wish you wouldn't talk like that to people. You're just making a fool of yourself. Can't you just be satisfied the way you are?"

I remembered the Benjamin Bogue Foundation course I had considered taking to help cure me. The literature now went into the wastebasket. I had enrolled in a different program—one that had a 100 percent success rate.

As the weeks passed, I continued to confess my healing. Oh, yes, there were doubts. Every so often someone would throw in a barb. "You still saying that?" they'd say, not quite concealing a smile. "Then when are you going to stop stuttering?" But I was determined and no taunt would dissuade me.

It happened after six weeks. Beulah and I were sitting at the breakfast table. She had just baked a rich "funny-cake" and I was enjoying it with my coffee. She poured herself a second cup and sat down. As we started discussing the upcoming day's activities, Beulah's eyes began to widen. I stopped in the middle of a sentence.

"What's the matter?" I asked.

"Gerald, you're not stuttering! You've been talking—you've been talking normally! I *knew* there was something different . . . !"

My fork slipped from my fingers and clattered on the plate. "You're right! My tongue is free. *I'm healed! I'm really healed!* Oh, thank you, Jesus! I really am healed!"

We laughed and cried at the same time. I began to try out all the words and letters of the alphabet that had been hardest for me to pronounce. Now that it had happened I could hardly believe it was true. After twenty years of being a chronic stammerer, I was healed! I felt like a new man.

The next few days were spent finding all my friends and showing off my miracle. Although I was so excited I could hardly get all the words straight, they knew right off the bat this wasn't the same Gerald they knew before. And they didn't quite know how to take it.

Mom and dad were surprised and happy for me. Yet they and the rest of the family took a we'll-wait-and-see-what-happens attitude. Sometimes it's so hard to accept as reality something one can't explain in a logical way.

As soon as my tongue was free the rest of me began to free itself. Little by little I crept out of the shell which held me captive. As I told others about my healing and the faith in God that brought it, I grew bolder. People were interested in what I had to say.

I gave my first public testimony to our local youth group. These young people had known me as a stutterer and were amazed when I started speaking freely and clearly. They were eager to hear all the details. I'm afraid my first speaking opportunity suggested the possibility of my being a long-winded preacher. I went on for fifteen minutes—ten minutes longer than the allotted time. But I couldn't help it. I had a lot of making up to do and the dam that had burst inside me was not to be stopped.

6

Sanctified in the Hosiery Mill

I developed an intense desire to share my new-found faith with others. It was that desire that prompted Beulah and me to order our first bundle of gospel tracts from Herald Press. I felt I wasn't capable or educated enough to talk to an audience. I hadn't gone to Bible school and I still felt inferior to the average guy. Yet, as a twenty-one-year-old zealous Christian, I wanted to witness to others. So we started handing out at least 1,000 tracts every weekend.

Beulah and I invited another couple to go with us each Saturday night and we walked Philadelphia's bustling, bawdy Market Street. What an education we got! We walked past bars, adult theaters, and strip joints, thrusting a gospel tract into every hand that would open to receive it. Sometimes the leaflet was quickly dropped in the gutter, but most were stuffed into pockets for later reference. There were even those who were interested enough—or desperate enough—to stop and talk.

At first I was afraid of getting into a conversation. I was acutely aware of my Christian immaturity and embarrassed at the thought of not being able to give an answer to some questions. So I practiced on those who didn't seem to notice my bumbling ways—the drunkards and beggars. They were always very gracious to me and had all the time in the world. I'd give them the plan of salvation and get them on their knees, then we'd go to the nearest coffee shop and I'd buy them a hamburger and a cup of coffee.

Those inebriated winos were my Bible school teachers. Those dirty ghetto streets were my seminary hallways, and the cost of the tracts, hamburgers, and coffee was my tuition. And I learned plenty. Sometimes the hard way.

It was late one Saturday night when a hulk of a man swaggered up to me. Reeking of liquor, he leered down into my face.

"Hand over your wallet right now, or you'll get a shot of hot lead right through ya!" he commanded.

I froze. He obviously meant business. The hand in his pocket was closed over a bulge that looked an awful lot like a gun. And now he shoved it into my stomach. Struggling against panic, I somehow managed a split-second assessment of the situation.

The easiest and safest thing to do would be to do just as he demanded—hand over my wallet. It didn't have much money in it anyway. On the other hand, the wallet belonged to me and he had no right to take it. He would just spend the money on more booze. Besides, if he did shoot me I was ready to go. My heart was right with God. But I sure didn't care to go right yet.

I decided to give him what he asked for. But as I reached towards my back pocket I thought I'd at least try to give him some kind of Christian witness.

"Sir, do you realize what this means to your soul?" I asked, looking up at him.

Don't ask me why I said those particular words. They just came out. And the result of those words was a reaction I hadn't anticipated.

"Whaddaya mean? You think I'm a terrible bad sinner? Just because I've killed sixteen people in my lifetime. . . !"

Dear God, am I to be number seventeen?

"I'll tell you something else. Jesus Christ was the first bootlegger who ever walked on this earth! Sure! He turned water into wine, didn't he?"

I gulped. By this time he was waving his hands wildly and raving and ranting so loudly that he'd attracted quite a crowd. My wallet was still in my pocket and he'd forgotten about his gun. Continuing with his tirade, he began to talk to the crowd. Gradually he walked away, still trying to justify his actions.

The crowd drifted away and I stood alone. A peace enveloped me and I looked up. "Thank you, Jesus," I whispered. "Thanks for sticking around." The gaudy neon lights seemed to dim and the raucous sounds drifted away as I looked up at the stars. It was great to be alive.

Another time didn't turn out quite as well. In the process of conversing with someone I said the wrong thing. I was slapped to the ground. The strange but wonderful thing about it was that I felt no pain. In fact it felt good. All that was getting hit was the dead shell I lived in.

My confidence grew and I gradually became bolder. Beulah and I got up the nerve to stamp our name and address on the back of each tract. It was through one of those stamped tracts that I led my first "real" convert to salvation.

A neatly typed letter came in the mail one day. It was written by a college student who, after reading the tract he'd been handed, had some probing questions. I delved into my Bible and tried to come up with the answers as best I could. We eventually arranged a meeting and he quietly accepted Christ into his life. I was as thrilled as he was. Getting a sodden drunk down on his knees was one thing. But leading an educated young man in his right mind to the Lord was quite another.

It wasn't long before I had the opportunity to take another step. I became acquainted with a Brethren in Christ man who asked me a strange question. His name was Walten Bergey.

"Gerald, have you been sanctified since you became born again?"

"Sanctified? What do you mean by that?" I asked.

"Well, have you been filled with the Holy Spirit and sanctified?"

"Uh, sure. I guess so. Didn't I get that when I became a Christian?"

"No, not exactly," he replied. "Let me ask you a question. Do you find yourself doing certain things as a Christian that you know you really shouldn't do? Or do you still revert to your old nature once in a while and then have to ask God's forgiveness all the time?"

Oh dear, I thought. He's hitting the nail on the head, that's for sure. My big problem was my temper. I had to admit it. And Beulah was usually at the other end of it. My explosions had become less frequent since I'd been saved, but they still came. Dad had the same problem and he always blamed it on the "old German" in him. I just guessed I'd inherited it and had to live with it.

"Yes, I suppose I do still have some problems," I understated. "And even though I ask God's forgiveness all the time, I still feel bad and wish I hadn't let myself go."

"Well, brother, you need to be sanctified. Here, read these books and you'll understand what I'm talking about." He shoved a couple of books into my hands. "They're written by John Wesley and Charles Finney and they'll explain why you need this experience and how to get it."

I tucked the books under my arm and assured Brother Bergey I would read them.

I did read them. And I was convinced. This "second work of grace" was what I needed.

For the next two months I started an intensive program of prayer and Bible study. While my hosiery machines were running at the factory I'd sit and read my Bible, chapter after chapter. I'd memorize verses one after another. On my way home after the job I'd stop at a secluded spot for at least an hour to seek God for this experience. Now that I was a Christian I wanted everything I could get out of it. No halfway stuff for me.

In the process of my pursuit of sanctification, I felt compelled to make restitution for anything in my life I had not taken care of before. The lengths I went to were extreme but my mind wouldn't rest until it was done.

I raked through my past with a fine-toothed comb. Among my gleanings was something that had taken place when I was just a youngster. It popped into my mind and loomed darkly as I reminisced.

It had to do with a muskrat. A stolen muskrat. The scene came into sharp focus as I remembered. It was a cold, dank morning just after dawn and I panted as my little legs pumped through the wet grassy field down the road from my house. There just had to be a muskrat in one of my traps this morning! I'd set them just right around the little holes—and two dollars a pelt was a small fortune. Skidding to a stop, I quickly inspected the traps. Not a single muskrat. But upon closer inspection I noticed a little furry thing wriggling in my friend Jimmy's trap. And it was about to get loose. It had chewed its leg almost off. Too bad Jimmy would lose his pelt. But wait. What if—I hesitated momentarily, then grabbed a stick off the ground, circled all my traps around the muskrat and proceeded to poke at him with the stick. Sure enough, after I'd tantalized him a few minutes he frantically chewed his leg free and scampered out of the trap—right into one of mine! Gotcha now, little critter, I gloated. No sense in both of us losing him. Right, Jimmy? I ran back home, quickly skinned the animal and later sold the pelt.

It had been many years since I'd seen Jimmy and I had no idea what he was doing now. But that muskrat grew in my mind until it assumed the proportions of a cow and I knew what I had to do. I looked up his address, found him still living in the area, and wrote him a letter. I explained what had happened, told him I was sorry, and enclosed a check for two dollars. Feeling a lot better, I slipped the letter in the mailbox.

A few days later I received a phone call from my friend. I began to smile as I listened to his response to my letter. Jimmy had become a born-again Christian himself, and while he rejoiced at my conversion, he declined my two dollars.

I searched every nook and cranny of my past and uncovered other little skeletons. A towel I'd taken as a souvenir from a hotel on our senior high school trip to Washington, D.C. A twenty-five-dollar deposit on a car I'd kept when the potential buyer reneged. Different people I'd offended with my tongue or attitude. They all got calls or letters. It wasn't easy, but I didn't want any obstacles on my path to sanctification.

My efforts were finally rewarded. It was a spring day and as I prepared my hosiery knitting machine I set my mind on several Scriptures I'd picked out. Oddly, though, my mind wouldn't concentrate. In fact, I couldn't remember a thing. My head was like a block of cement. I decided it must be some evil force trying to frustrate me. I'd read somewhere that if something like this happened you could resist the devil in the name of Jesus. So I started doing it the best I knew how.

"Devil, you leave me alone! I command you in the name of Jesus to get away from me!" I repeated it again and again. Then I started thanking Jesus.

"Thank you, Jesus, for a clear mind. I stand on your promises and accept your peace. Thank you, Lord. . . ."

I knew some of the guys on the floor were eyeing me strangely, but little by little I was caring less and less.

By the time I had said, "Thank you, Jesus" for the third time, it hit. A ball of fire began to roar in the pit of my stomach and to send its flames up through my body. The whirring of my machines faded into the distance as Bible verse after verse paraded through my head. Not only did I recall the verses, but I understood their meaning. Scriptures that had puzzled me became crystal clear.

The fire continued to roar. As it burned, my spirit began to soar. Unspeakable joy welled up within my being and I trembled with sheer exuberance. As I exulted in this joy, a warm blanket of love was wrapped around me and I felt at one with almighty God. It was then that I heard a voice speaking to me. It said gently and powerfully, *This is perfect love.*

After about an hour, the fire gradually subsided, but as it did, my body seemed to rise. For the next two-and-a-half days I felt like I was walking two feet above the earth's surface. It was heavenly! I don't know how my ladies' nylon stockings turned out that day but they must have been blessed!

That experience changed me once again. I felt a totally new love for my friends and family. And the bubbling joy I felt deep inside gave me a whole new outlook on life. Even my temper outbursts became all but nonexistent. My wife especially appreciated that benefit. She was thrilled with her "new" husband. That is, until I started in on her.

"Beulah, you need to be sanctified too," I urged.

"Oh, dear, I don't think so. I'm really glad you got it but, well, I just don't think I need it," she'd reply.

"Sure you do. You may not need as many bad things dealt with as I did, but don't you want to get rid of that old self that keeps you from enjoying the full blessing of the Lord? Don't you want all God has for you?"

"Well, yes, I guess. It certainly has changed you. But I'm just not ready yet."

"Listen, Beulah, why don't you let me pray for you right now," I persisted.

"No, Gerald. Please don't. I just don't want you to now." This time she quickly turned her face away from me and started to sniffle.

I knew I'd said enough. But I couldn't understand her reaction. Why wouldn't she want the thrilling experience I'd received? She just didn't know what she was missing.

A few weeks later, Beulah found it. We were attending a Brethren in Christ Holiness tent revival in Hilltown,

Pennsylvania. After the evangelist, John Rosenberry, preached a stirring message about the "old man nature," an altar call for those desiring sanctification was given. I looked over at Beulah. She was weeping softly.

I touched her hand. "Shall we go? I'll walk with you—"

She nodded.

We walked to the front and knelt down. The preacher laid his hands on her head and she received the same glowing joy I had received. There was one difference though. A disturbing one. Beulah was trembling as if she were charged with electricity and her teeth were chattering. In fact, all the way home she could hardly talk because of the way her jaw seemed to vibrate.

That part of her experience worried me a little. That hadn't happened to me. I couldn't understand what was making her do it. But she certainly looked happy.

Now that we both had the sanctification experience, our zeal knew no bounds. People could see we had changed and we grabbed every opportunity to tell them what had happened. I even took the liberty of sharing my experience with my Mennonite Sunday school class. Unfortunately, the Sunday school superintendent wasn't nearly as thrilled as I was and he forbade me to talk about it again.

I was undaunted. Beulah and I delved into the Scriptures again, seeking revelations that would make us even holier.

Gradually, though, like so many newborn Christians, our enthusiasm diverted us off the main path and into a rut. Since we were members of the Mennonite church, we figured that becoming holier meant being model

Mennonites. So we decided to become all that—and more.

We looked up the church's rules and regulations and began adhering to every one of them; we followed them to the letter. We warmed the pews every time the doors opened and took part in every function.

Being somewhat rebellious young Mennonites before, we still had been wearing normal clothing. But now we donned the regulation garb that set us apart from the fashions of the modern world. In addition to her little white net prayer cap, Beulah started sewing long caped dresses in plain, dark, somber colors. Opaque black stockings and black shoes completed her outfit. She wore her hair drawn severely back into a knot at the nape of her neck underneath her head covering. Any kind of jewelry or makeup was totally out of the question. I had my suits adjusted in a way that would do away with the lapels. Actually, the lapels were just flattened, resembling a priest's frock. These also had to be in dark colors along with black shoes. No neckties were tolerated.

After we'd conformed to the Mennonite regulations for a period of time, I began to get restless again. We still must not be dressing plain enough, I reasoned. I tried to think of any possible way that would make us less worldly.

Beulah, I'm afraid, got the worst end of my eventual frustrations. Ordinarily, a Mennonite woman would wear her prayer covering as much as possible—always to church and when out in public. I demanded Beulah to wear hers at *all* times—twenty-four hours a day. (What if she wanted to pray in the middle of the night or out in the garden and didn't have her covering on?)

I even began to have visions of myself covered from head to toe in black. Maybe a long cape that would cover every inch of flesh would be pleasing to God. I could cut two holes in it so I could peek through, then wear dark sunglasses. That ought to do it.

As my little fantasy progressed, I began to see how ridiculous it was. Certainly being dressed a peculiar way wasn't going to make me holy. In fact, I'd seen lots of my conservatively dressed Mennonite friends who surely didn't act holier than anyone else. Some of them acted downright unholy.

Then it dawned on me. I was forgetting all about what the Bible taught about the grace of God. His grace was a gift to us—not something we merited through works. Our faith and trust in Him was all He wanted. Furthermore, I read in the Bible that "all our righteousnesses are as filthy rags" (Isa. 64:6) and also that "man looketh on the outward appearance, but the Lord looketh on the heart" (1 Sam. 16:7).

What a relief! It was so easy. God loved me just the way I was and as I learned more about Him, He would show me how I could please Him by adorning the inward man and not worrying so much about the outward.

When I shared my thoughts with Beulah I found she'd been thinking the same way. Although we still agreed to dress in the Mennonite way, we decided we wouldn't be bound to it. And if the Lord asked us to change in some way, we would be willing to.

"It always does bother me a little to be dressed like this when we go passing out tracts on the streets," Beulah added. "Instead of asking about Jesus, the people want to know what religion I am."

"Well, yes," I said. "I guess you're right. From now on I

think we could dress in regular clothes to go out witnessing. It's less distracting and maybe the people will look at the tracts rather than at us. I really don't think God would mind."

God continued to change us. And as He did we were beginning to chafe at the bit again. Our Christian walk seemed to have grown monotonous and routine after coming back down to earth from our sanctification experience. Things had settled down to the point where I was becoming restless. I was teaching summer Bible school in the Conshohocken Mennonite Church and sharing my testimony wherever I had the chance, but it wasn't enough for me. Lately, even my job at the hosiery mill was becoming unbearable.

The rest of my family noticed my restiveness. "What's wrong, Gerald?" mom would ask. "You're always wanting to do something. Can't you just be satisfied being normal like everyone else?"

"I don't know. What's 'normal' anyway? Being like you and dad? I just feel I'm supposed to be doing something else—something more for the Lord. But I don't know what it is."

Two weeks later I found out what it was.

7

Our Wanderings Begin

It came in the form of a letter from my Uncle Llewelyn, the missionary in northern Minnesota.

"Gerald, I've been hearing some good reports of what you're doing—handing out tracts, having prayer meetings in your home. I'm going to suggest something I'd like you to consider. How about you and Beulah coming out here to help us on the Indian reservation? We certainly couldn't promise you much financially. But I will say we won't let you starve."

Something leaped within me. I distinctly remembered that nine-year-old boy sitting on the hard wooden church pew, hearing that voice telling him he'd be a missionary someday. The pennies and nickels I'd saved were long gone but the seed in my heart still waited to be fertilized.

I folded the letter carefully and laid it on the kitchen table. Was this really an answer to my prayers? Was this the reason I'd felt so unsettled with my job lately? Would I be willing to give up that job and the security it provided along with all the material possessions we'd accumulated? And more importantly, I wondered if Beulah would be willing to make the sacrifice with me.

My wife, her belly swollen with our first child, was resting in the bedroom. She opened her eyes and smiled when I walked in.

"Beulah, how would you like to be a missionary?" I asked cautiously, trying to be sensitive to her initial reaction.

She propped herself up on her elbow and looked at me to see if I was joking. "What? What are you talking about?"

"How would you like to go to Minnesota?" Might as well plunge right in and give her the whole thing at once, I reasoned. "Beulah, I just got a letter from my Uncle Llewelyn and he's invited us to come out to help him on the Chippewa Indian reservation." Even as I was saying those words I found myself beginning to plan our journey. This was what we were to do and I was sure of it. "I know we'd have to give up our house and car and I'd have to quit the factory—"

"Wait a minute, Gerald," Beulah interrupted. "Have you forgotten something? I'm going to have this baby sometime soon, you know. Do you realize what that means? It's not just the two of us any more. There'll be diapers and bottles and formulas—and what about a job? We'll need something to live on, won't we?" she added.

"Listen, Beulah. I know it would be a big step for us," I replied, "but, honey, I really feel this is an answer to our prayers. I just feel I need to be helping people in some way and what we're doing now just isn't enough for me."

"But, Gerald, I don't know if I like the idea of having our baby way out there in the sticks. Why, we'd be twenty-five miles from the nearest town, wouldn't we?"

I thought for a minute, then put my arms around her shoulders. "Beulah, I really feel this may be what God wants us to do. And if you'll be willing to go, we'll wait till the baby comes. How about that? I'll have to give notice at the job anyway. And we'll need some time to get everything in order. What do you think? Think we could do it?" I was trying hard to conceal my growing excitement. I knew she was beginning to see how much this meant to me.

A tremulous smile crept across her face. "Well, if you really think this is what we should do, I guess it's okay. I just hope you're really sure."

"Oh, I am sure," I answered as I gently stroked her hair. "You're a great wife really! I'll work everything out, so don't worry."

"You know what everyone's going to say, Gerald. They're going to think we're crazy. And your mom and dad—oh, I hate to think of what they're going to say—"

"Since when do we care what people say, huh?" I said nonchalantly. "Don't worry. I'll take care of it."

From that day on we began our preparations for the move that would change our lives. I immediately wrote back to my uncle telling him we would be coming and we set the date for our departure, July 2, 1951. I gave notice at my job and we started telling our friends and relatives. I found that Beulah's perception was right. Everyone *did* think we were crazy. Most of our close friends and relatives were deeply concerned. Just moving out of the community was a big step for a young Mennonite family in those days. But giving up a good job and taking your family way out to the north woods of Minnesota was quite another.

"Gerald, are you sure you know what you're doing?"

"How are you going to make a living for your family? You have to eat, you know."

"Don't you think you could be a witness in the hosiery mill as well as anywhere else? At least you'd be able to support your family."

"Yes, I guess I could," I'd reply. "But since I feel God has called me to be a missionary to the Indians, I'm sure there are plenty of sinners who can make ladies' nylon stockings. Don't worry. God will take care of us. You'll see."

My mother was aghast.

"Gerald, I just don't understand why you have to do this. Why can't you just be normal like the rest of us? Why do you have to be so serious about all this? Just think of your wife, and a baby on the way yet—why there's no telling what could happen out there with no conveniences and those wild Indians—" She always imagined the worst.

Our brothers and sisters were equally dubious. But our minds were made up and no one was going to dissuade us. My uncle wrote and although we first thought we'd have to sell most of our possessions, he said he'd found a house large enough to allow us to bring our furniture. There happened to be a creamery truck that made a regular trip to Minneapolis from our town to pick up butter. We arranged to have our furniture transported in that creamery truck. And to our delight, they agreed to take our belongings beyond Minneapolis all the way to our destination—an additional 225 miles. I sold my almost-new car and bought a four-wheel-drive Willys Jeep.

Beulah gave birth to our daughter, Joanne, on May 7, 1951. Six weeks later we rigged up her buggy in the back of the jeep and loaded all our possessions and bid a tearful farewell to our friends and family. With childlike faith, $200 and blissful ignorance of the road ahead, we plunged into the next chapter of our lives. Oh, what a wise Father we have to disclose His future plans only one step at a time. All He asks is that we take that step and trust Him for the next.

A few days later we bounced up the three-mile, rutted gravel lane to our new home. We'd prepared ourselves for the very worst so when we took our first look at the small, old Indian shack it didn't look so bad. The exterior was plastered with gray asphalt shingles and it was almost two stories high. It was complete with an outside pump and outside "bathroom." Of course it would be a little difficult to get to either. The grass was at least three feet high all around.

The Keller Creamery truck pulled up to the house behind our jeep and the driver stepped out. He walked over and leaned into the window of the car.

"Well, Gerald, you sure you want your furniture dropped off here?" A smile played around his mouth. "Sure looks like it could use some fixin' up, don't it? Well, at least the traffic won't keep you awake at night."

I ignored his dry attempt at humor. "Yeah, that's for sure. I guess we have a little work to do."

Beulah was silent as she stared at her new home.

"Come on, let's see what it's like inside," I said, as I climbed out of the jeep and stretched my legs.

Beulah lifted Joanne out of her buggy and we let ourselves into the house. A cold, dank draft slapped us in the face as we opened the door.

"Oh, dear," my wife grimaced, "just look at this mess."

The old Indian who'd been the former tenant had left everything as it was. A few sticks of battered furniture lined the walls and there were dirty dishes and pans left in the cupboards. It was filthy. Thick films of dust covered everything and a pungent odor told us there was spoiled food nearby. There was one small bedroom, a kitchen, and living area off the kitchen that we called a living room. There was a fifty-gallon-drum barrel stove we could use to heat the place.

"Go ahead and start unloading our stuff. I'll be out in a minute," I called to the truck driver.

We set our minds and bodies to the task before us. It was a good thing neither one of us was afraid of hard work. I immediately started to cut down the high weeds and brush that surrounded the house. In the process I killed a total of twelve snakes!

A scream from Beulah sent me running to the house only to discover she'd been surprised by a friendly snake in the mud-floored cellar. Later on, I bought a few goats to keep the grass down.

After the house had been scrubbed and furnished, Beulah suggested we find a suitable place for a garden. After all, food was a basic necessity and if we were going to live by faith we wanted to at least have some food in our stomachs.

Meat wouldn't be a problem. There were plenty of lakes around the area. I'd have to learn to be a fisherman. And the woods around the house were teeming with wildlife. I already knew how to trap muskrats. Getting milk for the baby wouldn't be a problem either. Our nearest neighbors down the road had a dairy farm and agreed to sell us fresh milk.

That first year was a real eye-opener as my little family literally lived off the land. Any romantic notions we may have had dissolved into the wind. I knew the $200 I had brought wouldn't last forever so we used it very sparingly. Uncle Llewelyn took me along as he helped the local Indian families build cabins and learn how to cultivate gardens. We'd earn their trust and then bring them to Sunday school at the little mission church so they could learn about God. It was arduous and dirty work with few obvious results and there were many discouraging moments.

But amid the hardship, I had that deep-down calm of knowing we were in the Lord's will. There was a great sense of fulfillment in helping these poverty-stricken people and for the first time I felt a real purpose in life.

Our first crisis came just a few weeks after we'd settled in. Beulah had tucked little Joanne in her crib for the night and we were almost asleep when we were startled by an ugly, throaty cough coming from the baby. Neither of us moved at first, but when the hoarse, hacking cough sliced the stillness again Beulah was on her feet.

"Oh dear, that sounds awful," she worried, slipping on her robe and slippers.

"Sounds like she has a cold or something," I answered sleepily.

A few minutes later Beulah came padding back over to the bed. "The baby doesn't seem right, Gerald. I noticed it earlier today. She seems to have a little fever too."

The ugly coughing began again and Beulah hurried over to the crib to pick the baby up. She wouldn't stop coughing.

That was the beginning of a six-week bout with what was later diagnosed as whooping cough—a dangerous illness for such a young infant. It climaxed one afternoon late that summer. The baby's cough had gone from bad to worse and resulted in spells that wore out her little body and left her gasping for breath. Beulah and I were up all hours of the night pacing the floor afraid to lay the baby down. Several times she'd almost choked to death as the strangling cough convulsed her body.

Beulah finally took her to the doctor, twenty-three

miles away in Detroit Lakes, but there was little he could do. We had to wait it out. As her condition worsened, our prayers intensified.

Finally, one afternoon Beulah laid the baby down in her crib and began to make applesauce in the kitchen. I was outside working in the garden. All at once I heard Beulah call in a frantic voice.

"Gerald! Gerald! Come here—the baby's choking, hurry!" Her voice ended in a shriek. I sprang to my feet and sprinted to the house. The sight I beheld sent a chill down my spine.

Joanne's mouth gaped open, her eyes were squeezed shut, and her tiny arms and legs flailed the air as she struggled for breath. In the sickening silent moments that followed, I watched helplessly as her color turned from bright pink to bluish-purple. Finally, the thrashing stopped and her little limbs went limp.

Beulah was beside herself. "Oh, Gerry, *do something.* She's going to die! Hurry, do something! O God, please don't let her die!" she wailed.

All of a sudden I remembered something that sent me running to the water pump. Uncle Llewelyn had told me when he was at our house once that if Joanne ever started choking and couldn't get her breath to get some ice water and douse her with it. I frantically jerked the pump handle up and down as I filled the old bucket with icy water, then dashed to the house.

Vaguely noticing the baby wasn't breathing, I recklessly splashed the water over her face and head. She gasped and squeaked, then let out a lusty yell.

"Oh, thank God," Beulah sobbed as she hugged the little girl to her. "She's breathing. Oh, I thought she was gone."

"Me too," I admitted, sighing with relief. In fact, I had

already visualized a funeral service. "You know at the last minute I just remembered what Llewelyn told us to do in case something like this happened. Thank God!" I felt like crying too.

That night after Beulah had lulled the baby to sleep and placed her in the crib, I tiptoed over and stared at the peaceful, tiny bundled-up form. Her blonde, feathery locks framed her pink cheeks as she breathed easily. Looking down at her in the darkened room I could hardly believe we'd almost lost her just a few hours ago. I carefully reached down and straightened her blanket. It was funny. I never realized how much I really loved that little person before.

8

"Into Your Lap the Lot Falls"

A few months passed and Indian summer, nature's consolatory gesture for the bleak winter ahead, was upon us. Our woods were aflame with hot oranges, reds, golds and a range of hues in between. The lush green rolling hills gradually turned brown along with the wide round faces of the sunflowers nodding in the fields. Although the sun shone with a piercing brightness through the dazzling azure sky, its daily appearance grew shorter with each passing day. Already some of the local Chippewa men had gotten themselves thrown in the town jail so they could at least be warm and fed there all winter.

Our $200 had gradually dwindled down to almost nothing. My uncle had assured us we would not starve and he was right—we always had food on the table. I'd winnowed out the best fishing spots on a few nearby lakes, but even the tastiest largemouth bass or northern pike can lose their flavor when they're on the menu day after day. Our little garden, rooted in the rich, black earth, was thriving and Beulah had even managed to can some peas, beans, corn, pickles and raspberries. But we were beginning to wonder where our gas money and milk money and the money it took for all other items was going to come from. On top of that, Beulah had begun to hint that she "sure could use a nice freezer" to preserve more food for winter. She was handy on the sewing machine so we weren't short of warm clothes. But shoes and boots presented a problem. Upon taking stock of our situation I decided to try and find a job. There certainly weren't any hosiery mills on the reservation, so that was out.

By this time I had developed a real love for the people in the community and my true desire was to have some way of earning money that would allow me to visit with the people. Lo and behold, I was presented with a job that gave me just that.

It just so happened that the local Watkins salesman had been reassigned to a different territory and he needed someone to take his route. It was the perfect job for me.

For the next three years I earned my living going from door to door selling Watkins products—ointments, spices, and salves. My salary was paid not only in cash but in chickens, potatoes, and sweet corn. Every customer along my route became a friend. I usually spent more time chatting over coffee and cookies than selling vanilla extract, but I soon had enough paying customers to make it worthwhile. And one by one they would venture into the little church. Then one by one they would accept Christ and sometimes even join the church.

I found it was relatively easy to bring people into the church, but it was more of a problem when it came to actual membership and becoming a Mennonite. There were just too many stringent rules and regulations, not to mention the dress code.

Although Beulah's hints for a deep freezer had become increasingly more frequent, we still couldn't seem to fit it into our budget. As fall set in she wanted to freeze some of the fresh vegetables and fruit. We decided to make it an urgent matter of prayer.

We prayed seriously but nothing happened. We just couldn't seem to make ends meet. Then gradually something occurred to us. All our lives we'd been taught to tithe, to give 10 percent of our earnings to the Lord. However, since we'd become missionaries we'd slacked up on our tithing, thinking we were already giving 100 percent of ourselves to the Lord's work. We just couldn't afford to give the money and besides it didn't seem necessary. Now I began to feel we had made a mistake.

So I tithed the last twenty-dollar bill we had to our names. And Beulah got her freezer.

Both our birthdays fall within a week in mid-October. That year, unbeknownst to us, our friends in Pennsylvania decided to surprise us with a card shower. And tucked into those greeting cards was money totaling $200—freezer money! On top of that, we received a telephone call out of the clear blue that our names had been selected at random from the local telephone directory and we had won $100 toward a major appliance of our choice. How wonderfully He supplies our needs! We were made freshly aware of the meaning of the words in Philippians 4:19, and we never again neglected to give God what was required of us, at least 10 percent. We couldn't afford *not* to.

Accustomed now to life in the wilds, Beulah had finally let Joanne down on the floor long enough to learn to walk. The wood-burning barrel stove in the kitchen would get red hot and heat the immediate area but the floors were always freezing in the winter. When something was spilled, it turned to ice before we could wipe it up. And there was always a coating of ice on the drinking water pail in the morning.

My Watkins route provided us with a living, but just barely. Therefore, we jumped at the chance to make a little extra one summer when someone mentioned there was good money to be made digging potatoes. We went fifty-five miles away to the heart of the Red River Valley. I'd worked on a farm before so I knew the potato harvest was hard work. But it was just for three weeks and I'd heard it said there was upwards of forty dollars a day to be earned. I figured we could use a little change of scenery anyway. What I didn't know was that besides earning money I would be taking another semester in "God's seminary."

Our living quarters for the next few weeks turned out to be an old weather-beaten chicken house which we shared with a few other families. Beulah wasn't exactly thrilled when we were shown to our corner of the large, drafty, musty-smelling room. But in her typical feminine way, she wasted no time beginning to tack blankets to the rafters for privacy and arrange a few vegetable crates to give the place a reasonable semblance of home.

"It shouldn't be too bad," she said gallantly. "We'll be going home on weekends anyway."

"Sure. And just think of all the different people we'll meet here," I hastened to add as I trailed my fingers through the thick dust on the windowsill.

After depositing Joanne with a couple of older girls who were baby-sitting with the youngsters while the parents worked the fields, we strapped large bushel-sized sacks to our backs and started picking up the uncovered potatoes. Up one row, down the next, we crouched along hour after hour. It didn't take long before nagging pains and aches developed in our necks, made their way down our backs and lodged in our legs. By the end of the day we were barely able to ease our stiff bodies onto our cots.

Besides all the human beings inhabiting our chicken-house home, we shared our quarters with other various creatures who seemed to come alive at night. Beulah and I were just drifting off to sleep one night when all of a sudden she jumped and screeched.

"O-o-ooh, there's something under the covers!"

Something furry skittered across my legs and I made a few wild grabs. Finally my fingers closed tightly over a little warm, squeaking bundle of fur. I hopped out of bed and with a churning stomach suffocated the mouse in my hand, then threw it out the door. Despite our tired, aching bodies, sleep eluded us a little longer that night.

Three weeks we spent picking potatoes. And in those weeks God didn't waste any time in giving me the opportunity to share with the other workers. We ended up having prayer meetings and we led several to salvation during that time.

Our little mission church was growing. Other members of my family had decided to move from Pennsylvania to be with us—my parents and Durell and his family were active members in the church. Dad got a job in town doing some free-lance painting and also kept some sheep fenced in behind their house. Durell was able to get a job in a body shop also in Detroit Lakes.

More and more people were becoming involved in the church and my part in the leadership was expanding. I had begun teaching from the Bible in a simple way and the people seemed to enjoy it.

As each week passed I felt more impressed that I was destined to be the pastor of this church. And when the time came for a new pastor, the general consensus of the congregation confirmed my desire. An informal vote by written ballot was unanimous in my favor.

However, the bishop over our district felt I was still quite young and a novice in the faith. He, therefore, decided to invoke the customary "lot method" of choosing a pastor. This was the conventional approved procedure for appointing the pastor of a Mennonite congregation in those days, a practice which had been instituted in the early days of the church. It is based on the Scripture in Proverbs which states "The lot is cast into the lap; but the whole disposing thereof is of the Lord" (Prov. 16:33).

I submitted to the bishop's decision although inwardly I didn't think he was giving me enough credit in light of the fact the congregation had already sanctioned me. However, I knew in my heart that I was to be pastor and that God would somehow work it out.

So on a Sunday night, another young man, surprisingly near my own age, was brought in as my contender. He just happened to be the son of a bishop and was much more educated than I, but I knew he didn't have the burden for this particular congregation like I had. In fact, I'd heard he had the reputation for being slightly frivolous and volatile and I wished they had picked someone else.

The church was full that night. The bishop was there to officiate while the other young man and myself sat on the front pew waiting for the proper time. Finally we were called up to the pulpit. Two Bibles lay on top. A small slip of paper had been placed in one of those Bibles and whoever picked the Bible that had the "lot" inside was considered God's choice.

The bishop asked the congregation to bow their heads

while he offered a prayer for God's will and direction. I remember feeling nervous and self-conscious as I tried to concentrate on his prayer. It still didn't seem right that we had to go through this.

". . . in Jesus' name we pray. Amen." The bishop looked up at me. "Brother Derstine, you may have the first choice." He nodded towards the Bibles on the podium.

I paused as I stared down at the two books. At least I had first choice. Not that it mattered. God was supposed to give each of us the right one anyway, no matter who was first. I reached out for the one on the right and slowly grasped it. My contender picked up the remaining one and, without opening the Bibles, we returned to our seats. The die was cast. I was aware of a stiff sensation in my arm which had picked up the Bible.

The bishop walked over to where we sat and we handed him the Bibles. I held my breath as he silently opened the one I handed him. It was empty! A stab of disappointment went through my chest and clung there as I watched him pull the lot from the other man's Bible. I had lost. For reasons known only to God, I had chosen the empty Bible. I was barely aware of the rest of the service. Afterwards I dreaded having to face my friends and family. Why had He instilled such a love within me for these people only to hand over their leadership to an almost complete stranger? I couldn't understand it.

I found out almost immediately that the rest of the congregation didn't understand it either. In fact they weren't happy about it at all. Some of them declared they would leave and go elsewhere rather than have someone other than me as pastor. I hastily encouraged them not to do anything so drastic, but just to trust the Lord to do what He thought best. In time I was sure we would understand His reasons.

My arm was actually painfully stiff for days afterward. I fought off the profound disappointment and dismay and attempted to adjust to the situation. It was extremely difficult to do, especially in the presence of sympathetic friends who felt obliged to keep reminding me of the unfairness of the procedure. Yet I never lost the original feeling I had about being pastor of that work. And it was that comforting, unassailing assurance that sustained me.

Six months later the bishop returned and offered to ordain me outright as pastor. He must have known the congregation wasn't satisfied with the one he had installed earlier, but I don't know the exact reasons he had for reversing the decision. It didn't matter. I was utterly elated to finally be able to step into the shoes that had been made to perfectly fit my feet. I had grown somewhat wiser for having waited patiently those six months. That was the summer of 1953.

It took me awhile to believe I really was pastor of the Strawberry Lake Mennonite Church. In some ways I felt terribly inadequate, but I was tremendously happy and felt humbled that God had placed me in this position. Of course, a little mission way up in the north woods of Minnesota might not have seemed like a conquest to some—and I still had to keep my Watkins route since being pastor wasn't a paying job. But I had a burden for these people, most of whom had joined the church through my contact with them over a cup of coffee and Watkins salves laid out on the table.

Soon after I was ordained, Grandpop Kaufman approached me. He was an elderly, retired farmer who lived in that area and had taken a special liking to our family. He spent many hours visiting and delighting baby Joanne with a peculiarity that gave her a certain eerie fascination. He had a glass eye he was able to pop out.

"Say, Gerald, I've been thinking. This little house you're living in don't befit a preacher," he started.

"Oh, it's all right," I answered. "It'll do till the Lord gives us something better."

"Well, I wanna put something to you. You know that little cabin I live in? Several years ago I had a dream, and in this dream I saw a piece of land. It was up on a hill with trees all over. It just so happened I was looking for a place to build a summer cottage, and after that dream I started looking for that hill. Well, you know, I found that hill and built me a couple of cabins on it. As you know, it's only a quarter mile from the church."

I nodded. "Yes, it is a beautiful spot. You have forty acres there, don't you?"

"Yuh. Now look, Gerald," he shifted in his seat and ran his hand over his bald head. "Now that you're pastor of that church you need a better place to live. I feel I should deed my forty acres to the church in your name. All you have to do is build yourself a home, a parsonage on it and write in the contract that if you ever leave this church you'd pay $500 to the Mennonite mission. Otherwise, the house would be yours."

I was flabbergasted. Beulah was expecting our second child and lately we'd been contemplating how nice it would be to have a bigger place. But it was just an impossible dream. Now it looked as though the Lord was going to give us our dream.

But how in the world would we be able to afford the

building costs of a new home?

God just happened to have that all worked out too. It seems a group of young people, our friends from Pennsylvania, had made plans to make the long journey to Minnesota to build us a home! They hadn't even heard about the land given to us. They just felt led to give some of their time and energies to the Lord and this was their way of doing it in a practical way. Five young men came and other friends who weren't able to come sent money for building materials.

What a happy time we had as our little home took shape! Grandpop Kaufman appointed himself contractor and supervisor. First, a spot was selected well off the road and then trees were felled as we carved out room enough for the house and garden. A full basement went in with a corner of shelves for Beulah's canning and an iron wood-burning furnace. The first floor consisted of an airy kitchen, living room, and bedroom, and the second floor had room enough only for two small bedrooms. We even had enough building materials left over to build a small bathroom—about 150 feet away from the house. But it was a nice one. Two smooth-rimmed holes and an old Sears catalog.

We moved into our little "mansion" in the fall of 1953, just in time for the birth of our son, Philip Gerald, on November 4. In honor of the events, we pressed Joanne's little hand print and baby Philip's footprint into the still-soft cement steps leading to the front door.

Although the church had grown considerably, I was aware of many people in the community who were unbelievers; several of them were atheists. Besides Indians, there were many Scandinavians—Finns, Poles,

Swedes, and Norwegians. These people had come from their countries seeking to be free from any kind of religion. I developed an intense burden for them. I expressed my feelings to my assistant pastor and we decided to pray earnestly for revival. For the next year we met at each other's homes from 5:30 to 6:30 every morning and fasted every Wednesday and Friday till three o'clock in the afternoon, the ninth hour. I had read somewhere that the early Christians did this. The congregation joined us in fasting and praying for revival.

The last week of December, 1954, a tiny flame leaped alive and began to burn. Revival walloped us in the face.

9

The Sparks Are Ignited

And he will cause to come down for you the rain, the former rain, and the latter rain in the first month. (Joel 2:23)

It happened during the Christmas holiday season—the last week of December and first week of January, 1955. A phenomenal chain of events that would radically change my life and eventually end up affecting the entire world had begun.

My wife and I, along with ministers from seven different Mennonite churches in Minnesota and Wisconsin, had organized a vacation Bible school during that holiday week at the Loman Mennonite Church, located about 200 miles from our place. Seventy-three young people enrolled, including some of those from my own church. I was to be moderator of the school.

On opening day we were alarmed to find that fourteen of these young people were unsaved. They had come for a good time and posed a potential problem to the school's success. As a body, we leaders decided to make their salvation a matter of fervent prayer.

"We only have five days," one of the teachers reminded us. "I don't know about you, but I'm willing to fast my meals to see these young people saved during this school."

"Yes, I would too," another teacher volunteered, "and if they'd accept Christ during the first part of the week they'd be able to get something from the teaching the rest of the week."

I decided to participate in the fast. I figured the longest we'd have to go was five days and I wouldn't starve in that time.

"I'll join you," I chimed in.

We joined hands and agreed not to touch food until those fourteen were saved.

The first day nothing happened, and our misgivings were right. Those teen-agers were already showing signs of rebellion and unruliness.

But the second day we rejoiced when one of the fourteen, a young fifteen-year-old, Skip, gave his heart to the Lord. And as a result of his glowing testimony the very next day the remaining thirteen were born again.

Needless to say, we had a changed school.

Early on the fourth morning, we got our first indication that this group of teen-agers was going to be different from what we'd anticipated. A few of the newly saved boys came running up to me as I walked to the church to start the morning classes.

"Rev. Derstine, guess what happened last night," one of them began breathlessly. "You'll never believe what we heard—"

"We heard *angels* singing!" another boy finished.

"Really, we *did!* It sounded like a choir, a really beautiful choir—"

"Yeah, it was outside our window. We looked out but didn't see anyone. That's how we know it was angels!"

"Man, it was some beautiful singing!"

I looked at them closely to see if they were trying to pull something over on me. They sounded sincere and I knew they'd just been saved so I just smiled and said, "Really? H'm-m-m. Well, that's nice. Come on in and let's find our seats."

Angels singing? They must have been dreaming. But all of them dreaming the same thing? Were they putting me on? I surely didn't want to discourage them. But there must be some logical explanation, I mused to myself.

The spirit was high in the school that day. I suggested to the teachers that we take all the students who wanted to go to International Falls for a street meeting during that afternoon's recreational time. From the way they were acting I was sure they would enjoy singing and handing out tracts.

The teachers agreed, so I presented it to the class. Immediately, all seventy-three hands shot up. They all wanted to go. I was a little surprised.

We arrived at International Falls later that day and we designated four of the older boys to go into all the beer joints and honky-tonks to hand out gospel tracts while six of the older girls were assigned to go into all the department stores downtown and do the same. Four others were just to walk up and down the sidewalks and hand out tracts to everyone they met. The rest of us would stand in front of the J.C. Penney store and sing gospel hymns and Christmas carols.

There was an unusual intensity and liveliness in the young voices that day, in spite of the biting wind and blowing snow. Not long after we started singing, the manager of the store came out.

"Why don't you come on in where it's warm? You can

all go up on the second floor where there's a balcony. Your singing sounds very nice."

We didn't need a second invitation. Moments later we were trooping up the steps. I lined the young people up in front of the balcony railing and we began singing. "Joy to the World" and "Victory in Jesus" rang out in exuberance. Their voices carried through the store and shoppers stopped dead in their tracks when they walked through the front doors.

After we'd been singing a short time, I felt a tap on my shoulder. "Rev. Derstine, do you think I could give my testimony?" It was one of the young girls who'd just been saved. She caught me a little off guard.

"Uh, well, I guess you could," I answered slowly. We weren't used to having testimonies in church, much less in a Penney's store. I was even surprised she knew what a testimony was.

The song ended and Theresa walked up to the railing and looked down at the people below with a smile.

"I've just accepted Jesus Christ into my heart and I want you to know what peace and joy I have. Oh, if you could only experience what I have and find that Jesus really loves you." She leaned over the railing and tears began to fall from her eyes onto the floor. She urged the shoppers to accept Christ as she had.

By that time I was beginning to feel a little uncomfortable and I was very glad when she finished. No sooner had she stopped, however, than someone else came and tapped me on the arm. It was a young man this time, another one who had just been converted.

"Rev. Derstine, I'd like to give my testimony too."

I paused a second before I nodded to him. "Okay, go ahead." He proceeded to do the same thing the girl had done.

Now all activity in the store had come to a standstill. All attention was focused on our little group. Even the clerks and office workers had come away from their desks to watch.

By the time I finally decided we'd gone long enough, three more had given their testimonies with the same intense and emotional fervor. And I was fidgeting. Sure, I was happy for these new Christians, but they seemed so overly emotional about it. Well, I figured, they were just teen-agers and entitled to be a little extreme. All the same, I didn't want to wear out our welcome with the store manager. I led the group in a final carol and we filed downstairs and safely outside.

That evening back at the school I decided to ask several of the young people to tell their impressions of the afternoon's activities. During the fifteen-minute devotional I normally conducted before the evening class, many of the local people attended and I thought it might be interesting to them.

"Who of you would like to give a testimony and share what happened in International Falls this afternoon?" I asked.

To my amazement all seventy-three hands reached for the ceiling.

"Oh, dear, we won't have time for *all* of you," I smiled. "But if you really feel what you have to say is sincere and important, I'll ask you to stand up where you are." This ought to eliminate most of them, I thought.

But to my astonishment they *all* stood up. Now what am I going to do? I certainly never expected this. One more try.

"Listen, we only have fifteen minutes, hardly enough

time for all of you. But if you feel you *must* say something and God really has something to say through you to the congregation, I'm going to ask you to remain standing, await your turn, then come up to the pulpit one by one to talk. The rest of you may be seated." This ought to do it!

But no one sat down! I couldn't believe it. Just then, a couple of the teachers walked over and in view of the circumstances offered to give up their part of the evening class for that night. After a hurried, whispered consultation, we all agreed to let the young people give their testimonies and forego the scheduled classes.

So, one by one, they filed up and told in their own way what Jesus meant to them and how they'd been blessed that afternoon. After about ten had given their testimonies, one of the young men walked up to the altar crying loudly. He was the first one of the fourteen who was saved.

He knelt down and I hurried to his side wondering what was wrong. "Skip, why are you crying?" I asked softly.

"Oh," he sobbed. "I want my mother and father to learn to know Jesus the way I have come to know Him."

An honorable enough reason to be concerned, I thought. I just wished he didn't have to be crying about it. Not in front of everyone in church. It wasn't normal.

Then I heard another muffled sob as a second boy, Ron, a fifteen-year-old Indian, came walking to the front. When I walked over and asked him why he was crying he also said he was burdened for his mom and dad.

At that point I figured I'd better do a little explaining to the congregation. I stepped behind the pulpit and calmly assured the audience that everything was all right and that these boys were just very concerned about their unsaved families. But when I glanced down at them again I noticed they were shaking violently and one proceeded to fall onto his back onto the floor. His eyes were shut and he seemed unconscious. Ron then fell on his back in the same manner.

God help us, I thought. What is going on? Has the devil gotten in here somehow? I didn't see how he could have with all the singing, testifying and Bible-quoting we'd been doing.

All of a sudden there was a clatter and a thump halfway back in the congregation. Every head turned in time to see a young boy who had fallen off his chair and was prostrate on the floor. His eyes were closed, and he was shaking violently.

By this time the meeting had come to an abrupt halt. Taking a quick evaluation of the situation, I came to the conclusion that the devil must have gotten in our midst somehow, so we teachers decided to take steps accordingly. Somewhere I'd read about being able to "plead the blood of Jesus" if a person was overtaken by an evil spirit. I asked one of the teachers to lead the congregation in prayer while I recruited several young people to help the rest of us.

We then circled ourselves around each person on the floor, put our hands on them and began repeating, "I plead the blood of Jesus, the blood of Jesus, I *plead the blood of Jesus!*"

As soon as we started doing that, though, the shaking and trembling not only didn't stop, but it got worse!

I heard another thud and a young girl up front slid off her chair to the floor. I was alarmed to see she wasn't shaking like the others. She lay deathly still. I quickly walked over to her and, as I stood looking, two of her girlfriends walked up to my side. They looked down at her, then over at me. "Rev. Derstine," one of them asked, "is-is she dead?"

"No," I answered reassuringly. "I'm sure she'll be all right." I doubt if I convinced them. I knew I hadn't convinced myself. But there was no way I was going to stoop down and take her pulse.

Then there was another thud. And another. Things were really getting out of hand now. We couldn't keep up with them and it seemed the more we pled the blood of Jesus, the more they shook. Pretty soon there were eight on the floor.

I hurried up to the pulpit once again and suggested we all sing, "There Is Power in the Blood." Several in the audience had already made a beeline for the back door. But the rest of them sang, not yet having the courage to leave their seats.

I just couldn't figure it out. How had the devil gotten in? We'd all been having such an unusually blessed day. All the young people had seemed so sincere and the spirit was so high. What had happened? I wished there weren't so many guests there that night. I could imagine what they were thinking.

Leaving one of the teachers to keep the congregation singing, I stepped down to help pray for those on the floor. To my dismay, the situation was getting even worse. Now, one by one, their lips were starting to chatter and strange sounds were coming from their mouths. It sounded like another language.

All at once my mind started clicking. I'd read something about a pentecostal thing called "tongues." I had thought it was some kind of fanatical emotional thing that was practiced by weird people. When I was a little boy, mom would tell me about these people called "holy rollers." Whenever we went to the Perkiomenville Auction we had to pass by an Assemblies of God place called Eastern Bible Institute. That's where the "holy rollers" lived and mom said that sometimes these people would get so happy they would die. The school was at the top of a steep hill and I was always glad when we were on the other side of that hill. I'd sure hate to get a flat tire in front of that place and have some of those people come rolling down the hill to help us.

Just recently, though, a pentecostal man had cornered me and asked if I'd been "baptized in the Holy Spirit." I quickly said, "Yes," remembering my glorious sanctification experience.

"Did you speak in tongues?" he asked.

"Why no, I didn't," I answered.

"Well, then you didn't get the Holy Spirit," he shot back.

I argued with him. I *knew* I had the Holy Spirit and there was no way he could convince me otherwise. But lately I had been randomly picking up books that mentioned this experience—this "tongues."

Concentrating now on the situation at hand, I was debating my next moves when I noticed my uncle, the school's principal, walking toward one of the boys on the floor. He looked at the boy momentarily, then proceeded to pick him up by the armpits and to start dragging him toward the cloakroom. The boy was chattering all the way, still in a trance. I caught up with them.

"What are you doing?" I asked.

"I'm taking him out of the sanctuary, Gerald," he answered firmly.

"But why?"

"Well, I think they might be speaking in tongues and if they are I understand someone has to give an interpretation or else they're out of order. So we have to get them out of the sanctuary at least."

I felt sorry for him. He was the one with the most responsibility and he seemed so utterly helpless. He dropped the boy in the cloakroom and went back for another one.

But two others had fallen in the place of the one he'd dragged out. He carried a couple others out before deciding it was a losing battle. For every one he carried out, others would fall in their places. So he concentrated his efforts on those who were still up but looked like they might go down next.

By this time I was nearly beside myself with anxiety. I could picture ambulances, their sirens wailing and lights flashing, pulling up to the church door for these young people. What would we tell their parents? We had to do something.

I tried going around to each one, holding them still if they were shaking, or shaking them if they were holding still. Somehow we had to restore order.

Two hours later, in desperation I stepped out the side door for a breath of fresh air. I shut out the din behind me, took a deep breath and looked up at the stars.

"Dear God, please help us!" I pleaded.

10

Visitation From God

The little clock in the back of the church was ticking away, into the wee hours of the morning, when our first assurance came that this was indeed a work of God. Skip, the first boy who had come crying to the front, stopped the strange jabbering and began to speak intelligibly. A radiant smile lit up his face as he began to clearly articulate one word at a time. He spoke so slowly and so softly we had to lean close to hear what he was saying. His body was relaxed and peaceful now but his eyes remained closed as he said in a gentle, barely audible voice, "Turn—in—your—Bibles—to Acts 2:17—and—18—and—you—shall—under—stand—"

I quickly reached for my Bible. Thank God, at least he was saying something scriptural. My fingers trembled as I leafed through to the book of Acts, chapter 2, verses 17 and 18. I began reading to the small cluster of people who had gathered around the boy:

> And it shall come to pass in the last days, saith God, I will pour out of my Spirit upon all flesh: and your sons and your daughters shall prophesy, and your young men shall see visions, and your old men shall dream dreams: And on my servants and on my handmaidens I will pour

out in those days of my Spirit; and they shall
prophesy.

I stared at the words in astonishment. Then I looked at
the boy and back at the verses again. Could all this truly
be a work of God? In fact, could it be possible that this
was the very revival we had been praying and fasting for?
I wanted to believe it. Yet it was contrary to our doctrine.
We had always been taught that these particular Scriptures had been fulfilled in Bible days. I read over the
passage once more. "In the last days—"

"Brother Derstine! Come over here. Connie's saying
something." I hurried over to the side of the young girl
who was still lying on the floor. She also had a heavenly
smile on her face and was talking. She spoke authorita-
tively, one word at a time, as she told of an "end-time
revival" such as the world had never seen. Her friends,
hovering over her, leaned close to catch every word. On
their faces was a mixture of bewilderment and relief.

By that time the other young people who had been
lying on the floor, "speaking in tongues" and trembling,
became still and one by one they began to speak. Some of
them sang. Others described heavenly scenes complete
with elaborate descriptive gestures. Yet they all still lay
on the floor, eyes closed, in a trance. There were
prophecies of impending world events. (These particularly bothered me. We were only interested in revival for
our own community.) There were words of exhortation
and passages of Scripture. As each one ended his message
almost invariably he would say, "This is my body you
see, this is my voice you hear, but this is from the Lord."
One word at a time.

Uncle Llewelyn was bewildered. He, more than any of

us, didn't know whether to be happy or to become more upset. At least he was grateful the situation seemed to be a little more peaceful.

He walked over to another of the girls who was lying on the floor. Her whole face seemed illuminated as she described her vision of Jesus.

"He's got the kindest, sweetest face," she murmured. "And His hair—so soft. Here, Jesus, take my hand—" She raised her arm and grasped the air with her fingers. Tears trickled down her face and through her hair. From the look on her face there could be no doubt she was beholding the face of Jesus.

I walked over to Ron, the Indian boy. He too was speaking of the soon-coming of Jesus Christ. "The time is short," he was saying. "Jesus is coming very soon. Get your heart right with God and make your wrongs right with each other." His copper-hued face, framed by his straight, jet-black hair, was serious, intense and pleading.

I continued my rounds, elbowing my way through the small clusters of young people huddled around each person to hear what they all were saying. Even though I myself was being caught up in the exhilaration of it all, it was extremely important to me to make sure they were all doing or saying something that was according to the Bible.

Around midnight a particularly strange prophecy came through one of the boys. "There are two people here who have unconfessed sin in their lives. If you will humble yourselves and confess your sin, God will release you and bless you." The room quieted momentarily as each of us searched our hearts.

All at once I felt a light touch on my arm. I opened my eyes and saw it was Beulah. She was wiping tears from her eyes.

"Gerald, I am one of those two. Will you get Mark Landes to come and pray with me?"

After recovering from my surprise, I attempted to console her. Lord, I prayed, just comfort her and let her know she is forgiven. I couldn't understand what she could have done to make her feel this way and my heart went out to her. Brother Landes, one of the teachers, came over to pray with Beulah as she knelt on the floor.

When only a few minutes had passed, I heard Beulah begin to laugh. She threw her hands up in the air and with a glorious smile on her face she launched into a loud babble of tongues! I stared at her in shocked disbelief. This was my wife! Not one of the young people. Up to this time it was only the teen-agers who had been acting this way. I couldn't believe it. Surely this was an act of God. Beulah would never do this on her own. Never. In fact, she was always quick to criticize someone for "putting on a show."

That was Beulah's baptism in the Holy Spirit. And it was so complete that to this day she can't remember the sin that she asked God to forgive her for that night.

The hours wore on. Most of the young people lay on the floor for two to three hours before getting up and recounting magnificent visions of heaven or of angels or Jesus himself. As they came to, they wept and went from one to another asking forgiveness and expressing their love. Some even went to homes out in the community and got people out of bed in order to make their wrongs right. Tears flowed unchecked as arms were flung around necks and then raised in the air in thanksgiving to God. My own dazed wonderment eventually gave way to overwhelming joy and I allowed my own voice to ring out in praise along with the others. I now was convinced God had visited us in a strange and exciting manner.

Some of the Mennonite teachers had left long ago, but others were now raising their hands and with uplifted faces were praising God with a loud voice. Brother Bob and Brother Harvey, both teachers, had their arms and faces lifted and were sounding like religious fanatics but still looking like quiet, conservative Mennonites in their plain clothes. The scene was unbelievable, but seemed absolutely normal at the time. For once in our lives we were forgetting about everything except praising and glorifying God. Nothing else was important.

It was 5:45 the next morning when the last person left the church. Beulah picked herself up off the floor and, although she was still a little unsteady on her feet, managed to make it to our room. A peace and calm seemed to have settled over her and the glow hadn't left her face. I was almost afraid to touch her.

Thanking God for the previous evening's events, we went to bed for a couple hours. I had a class that morning at eight so we wouldn't get much rest. After climbing into my pajamas, I knelt down beside the bed and prayed.

"Lord, I do thank you for the wonderful things that happened in our midst. And yes, I do believe *you* were the one who was responsible, even though I don't really understand all that took place—or why it all took place. One thing, though. Just between you and me, I would kind of like to know what it's like to speak in tongues. That's what it was, wasn't it? Beulah got it and she seems so happy, so different, and well, being a pastor and all, it seems that I should experience it so I can understand better. But if you don't think it's necessary and you don't think it would be good for me, I'm perfectly happy without it. You understand that, God. I'm not going to ask for it again, so if you want to give it to me, okay. If not, that's fine too. Amen."

We slept for an hour or so and I awoke, strangely refreshed, and prepared for my morning class. In the full light of morning, the previous night seemed like a fantastic dream, like it wasn't even real. I was glad it happened, but now I was glad it was over. I didn't like the feeling of things being so out of control. Besides, I hated to think what impression the community people had received. I sure hoped they didn't think we did this all the time! We'd have to get things back to the regular routine today.

I let myself into the church, shut the door behind me, and stopped dead in my tracks. Two young people were sprawled out on the bare floor in front of me.

Oh, no, I groaned inwardly. Is this going to happen again today? It had been such a relief last night when all the boys and girls had gotten up and seemed all right. We didn't have to resort to ambulances and mental institutions and I was convinced it was a work of God. But all the same I wasn't anxious for it to happen again and seeing two on the floor this morning was a mild shock.

That whole day turned out to be a repeat of the night before. There was just no way we could stop it. It was like a boulder that had been pushed off the top of a mountain and rather than stopping, it was only to gain momentum. That day there were more unsettling prophecies and predictions of upcoming world events.

Young Ron spoke words which included the statement, "What is happening here has never happened like this before and will never happen again in this manner in the history of the world." Someone else gave a word about

Billy Graham, not so well-known in those days. This prophecy stated that he would be able to take the gospel behind the Iron Curtain. Several years later this prophecy was fulfilled.

Some of the young people spoke prophetically of a "renewal in the church" or an "awakening." This disturbed me. We weren't really that interested in a worldwide revival or even a renewal in our denomination. That was too big for me to comprehend. All we wanted was to reach needy people in the radius of our small church and give them the message of salvation. We were concerned about our community.

In fact, the Mennonite theology didn't coincide with what we were hearing. We had always been taught there would be a great "apostasy" or falling away in the last days as stated in 2 Thessalonians 2:3, not a worldwide revival.

Other prophecies given during that day were directed personally to different ones of us. In every case, when the person would come out of this trance-like state he would have no recollection of saying any words. All he'd remember was a beautiful vision or euphoric sensation. We'd have to tell him what he'd said! And to make things even more amazing, these young people had all come from small rural areas, some of them uneducated, and most of them totally ignorant of the Bible. Many of them had just been saved a few days so we knew it was miraculous when they quoted Bible verses and texts verbatim in this odd, one-word-at-a-time way.

At one point I heard my name called. "Gerald!"

I hurried over to the side of Ron who was lying on the floor.

"Gerald, the Lord says you shall not speak in tongues

today yet, but you shall soon."

I stared down at him, first embarrassed that he would know that I even desired that experience, then shocked when I remembered he had no way of knowing I had even prayed that prayer. I had prayed it to myself the night before, and not even my wife knew about it. I had told no one.

Well, I consoled myself, at least you don't have to worry about it happening to you today. That settles that. But a few minutes later I got another word.

"Gerald, you must be at your church at Strawberry Lake on Monday morning between six and eight o'clock. There will be two people waiting to meet you there."

That was all. No explanation of what they would want or why I had to be at the church on Monday morning. Nothing. But it didn't occur to me not to obey. I would be there.

Our Bible school ended on that note and we headed back to the Strawberry Lake reservation. I was glad the week had finally ended. I needed time to think over all the peculiar things that had happened in the past few days. They were wonderful days but my head was swarming with questions and I wished I could talk to somebody who could reassure me about what was going on.

Beulah packed our belongings into the car and bundled up the children as we prepared to drive back home that night. The air was as still and dark as the inside of a deep freeze and heavy white flakes of snow fell in silence. The young people we'd brought along with us crowded into the car with my family and after knocking the snow from my boots on the car's side I climbed in behind the steering wheel.

"Ready to go?" I announced.

"We're ready!" the voices chorused from the back seat.
"How 'bout turning the heater on. It's cold back here."
"Strawberry Lake, here we come!"
We set out for home, reminiscing about all the things
that had happened during the past few days. The baby
and three-year-old Joanne fell asleep and after a couple
hours of sharing, the rest of my passengers followed suit.
I cracked my window to let some of the frigid air blow
over my eyes.

All of a sudden a voice behind me erupted into the
unknown language that was now almost familiar. I
turned halfway around in my seat and saw Skip in the
darkness, his head resting on the ledge in front of the
rear window. As soon as the strange message ended he
began to interpret it. It was directed to me.

"Gerald, you are to be at your church on Monday
morning between six and eight o'clock. There will be
two people there to meet you."

The same thing I'd heard before—from another person!

The car became silent again until my little daughter
stirred from her sleep on Beulah's lap.

"Mommy," she began.

"Yes, dear," Beulah answered, opening her eyes and
adjusting the little girl on her knees.

"Mommy, I saw Jesus!" Joanne said, opening her eyes
wide and looking right at Beulah.

"You saw what, honey?" she asked.

"I saw Jesus!" Joanne insisted. "Look! There He is! Over
there!" She pointed in the darkness. "Can't you see Him?"
She paused, then chattered on excitedly.

"I was sitting on His lap and He was reading a bi-i-g
book to me. Had pretty pictures in it too."

Beulah and I exchanged glances. "How did you know it

was Jesus, honey?" she asked.

" 'Cause, I just know. He looked so purty," she answered.

"Didn't you see Him too?"

Beulah hugged her close. "No—but I would have liked to."

"Oh, I wish you could too. Maybe if I go to sleep again I will see Him again." She settled herself back down and closed her eyes.

I looked over at Beulah again. "Did she say she saw Jesus?" I whispered.

"Yes. Can you imagine?"

"Did she ever do that before?" I asked.

"No—she's only three and a half—" Beulah's voice trailed off.

"What is happening to us? This thing is even affecting the children." I didn't know if I liked that or not.

We dropped the young people off at their homes one by one, and again I found myself hoping this strange thing had come to an end.

Our first church meeting upon our arrival home was the regularly scheduled Saturday night young people's prayer meeting. Nothing unusual had happened all day Saturday and I figured it was safe to let some of the students tell what had happened at Bible school in Loman. As I walked into church that night I was pleasantly surprised to see the large crowd that had gathered.

Starting time approached and I stood up behind the plain wooden pulpit to announce an opening hymn. It was good to be back home again in comfortable, friendly surroundings. I noticed my dad sitting in his usual seat about halfway back.

Picking up the pitch pipe and smoothing the hymn book open in front of me, I said, "Please turn in your hymnal to—"

My sentence was abruptly interrupted by a heavy bump and thud. It was a familiar thud. My stomach did a flip-flop. Not again! Not *here!*

I put my song book down and hurried over to where the young man had fallen. He was shaking and talking in that strange tongue just like they had in Loman, 200 miles away. Several people gathered around the boy. It was no surprise to the ones who had just come from the Bible school. They just started praising the Lord.

Just then another thud echoed through the church and another boy crumpled between the benches onto the bare wooden floor. Soon after he fell the first boy's voice rang out in an authoritative tone.

"You must sing, 'Victory in Jesus'! "

By this time I'd figured out the direction the service was going to take and had resigned myself to it. It was useless to resist.

After singing that song it seemed as if the most intimate presence of God himself descended on the congregation. The meeting was almost a duplicate of what had happened in Loman as tongues, prophecy, and interpretation flowed like a rushing river. Prophetic words of direction to one another, about revival in the church, community, and the world were given. Sins were brought into the open and dealt with on the spot. We were instructed to pray fervently for the salvation of parents of the new converts and were given the assurance that they would indeed be saved. People began asking each other's forgiveness, making their wrongs right, and weeping on one another's shoulders. Someone would begin a song and it would be taken up wholeheartedly. The walls of that plain little Mennonite sanctuary resounded with melodic praise.

That meeting lasted and lasted and the little clock on the back wall was forgotten. It must have been around 1:00 A.M. when my dad was given some specific instructions. He was told to drive four miles away to the home of two sisters who had been a part of the Bible school and tell the unsaved parents to come back with him to the church. They were to receive a "spiritual blessing" to be revealed upon their arrival at the church.

What would have seemed a strange directive at another time seemed oddly normal to us. Dad got in his car and drove off to do as he was told. In the meantime another message came to us from one of those lying on the floor.

"Gerald, your dad will not be able to persuade these people to come to the church. You must go and tell them to come. You will pass your dad on your way there but do not stop to speak to him."

Obediently, I left the building, got into my car and headed for the Dodd's house. Sure enough, about halfway there I passed dad's car returning to the church. He was the only one in it.

When I arrived at the house the lights were still on and I nervously walked up on the porch and knocked on the door. When the girls' father and mother opened the door I smiled and tried to explain as simply as I could.

"Where are Joy and Louise?" Mrs. Dodd asked anxiously. "They left here hours ago, saying they were going to church. Willis tried to get us to come down there, but do you realize what time it is?"

They were trying to be nice. Ever since the girls had started going to church they'd had a lot less trouble with them but they themselves were not interested. However, they knew me well. In addition to being the church's pastor, I'd sat at their kitchen table many times with my

Watkins products spread out next to a cup of coffee.

"Yes," I said now. "I know it's very late but something highly unusual is happening at the church and God told us to have you come down and receive a spiritual blessing. Your girls are all right; you don't have to worry about them. I don't understand all that's going on but God is speaking through people that have fallen on the floor and well—just come. Won't you come and see for yourself?"

The Dodds looked at each other and then back at me. They were shaking their heads.

"Oh, no, I don't think we can come now. And furthermore you'd better tell the girls to come on home."

I should have known they wouldn't come. But why had God made me come down all this way at this time of night—for nothing? I thanked them for listening and left.

When I arrived back at the church things had broken up somewhat and people were getting ready to go home. But there was one message for Beulah and me. We were to take Joy and Louise home along with three others and when we got to the Dodds' house, we were to go in and have a prayer meeting!

Now I was really puzzled, and a little weary. It was two o'clock and after being interrupted twice in the middle of the night the Dodds weren't going to be too excited about us having a prayer meeting in their house.

Strangely enough, however, when we pulled into their driveway and escorted the girls to the door, we were all invited in! So we ended up having the prayer meeting the Lord told us to have, singing, reading from the Bible and praying together. And by the time we left, the Dodds had indeed received the spiritual blessing God had promised them and we left, comfortable in the fact that we had obeyed Him explicitly. It was now going on three o'clock.

But before we got to the car, Ron stopped dead in his tracks and started to talk in the now familiar one-word-at-a-time voice.

"Gerald, you are not to take me home. You are to take me to your house and we are to pray the rest of the night."

"Oh, no, Ron. You should go home," I argued. "Your parents will be terribly worried about you being out all night like this."

"You are to take me to your house," he said firmly. "And when you arrive at your house you will see that all your lights are lit."

Now that was really strange. Why would all our lights be on? There was no one there and we turned them out when we left. I was always careful about that. Furthermore, if they were on how would Ron know? He'd been at the church all night with us.

"What do you think we should do?" I whispered to Beulah.

"Well, why don't we go to our house first and see if the lights really are on. If they're not, we should just take Ron home."

"Yeah, that sounds good," I agreed.

A few minutes later we pulled into our driveway. Beulah gasped. "Look, Gerald! Our lights *are* all on. There must be someone in our house!"

"You're right. Look at the car—"

I drove up next to our front door, turned off my headlights and got out cautiously. All at once the door swung open and three young men bounded out.

"Hey, Gerald, hope you don't mind us makin' ourselves at home," they laughed.

I let my breath out slowly. It was Amos, his brother

Freddy, and Johnny. I knew them well. They were from my hometown in Pennsylvania and had all been with us at the Loman Bible school last week.

"Of course not," I said now, as we all walked into the kitchen. "You know you're welcome. But how did you get in? Wasn't the place locked?"

"Yeah, it sure was. But Johnny just climbed up the side of the house and opened the window in the upstairs bedroom."

"Then we figured you'd be home soon and thought we'd better turn all the lights on so you'd know someone was in the house," Amos continued.

"How long have you been here? Did you come right from Loman?" I asked.

"Oh, we've been here about an hour," Freddy answered. "We came here in kind of a roundabout way. We had some strange things happen to us though. It all started when we left—"

All of a sudden Ron collapsed onto the floor. I couldn't believe it. This was my home—not a church. These things couldn't happen here!

But Ron began to talk, his eyes closed. He told us in detail all that had happened to Amos, Freddy, and Johnny since we'd seen them last. He described the people they had met, the places they had visited, and further, the fact that they were here for a purpose and God was going to move here also.

When he finished I looked at the boys. They noticed the question in my eyes and said, "Gerald, all he said was exactly what happened. Exactly."

"Do you think this is going to start happening here too?" Amos asked a little too eagerly.

"I don't know, but it's late and I think we should all go

to bed," Beulah interjected. "You boys are welcome to sleep in the upstairs bedrooms."

"Wait, Beulah," I said. "Ron's still on the floor. Shouldn't we wait for him?"

Just then Ron called my name. "Gerald!"

I looked down at him. "Yes?"

"Turn to page eighty-seven in the hymn book on your piano and play three verses of that song."

Talk about strange! I hesitated, looking over at Freddy. "Why in the world would he say something like that?" I asked.

"I sure don't know," Freddy replied. "God must be talking through him. You better go do what he says."

Feeling slightly foolish, I walked over to the piano, picked up the hymn book and leafed through the pages to number eighty-seven. The song was: "Savior, Thy Dying Love." I sat down on the bench and started playing the song. I'd never played it before but I remembered the tune. Its sweet, haunting melody accompanied words that told the story of the Crucifixion. I remembered it being sung at funerals and now as I played in the wee hours of the morning it sounded infinitely sad.

Before I had barely finished the first verse, Amos began to sob. His big shoulders heaved as the tears rolled down his face. The more he cried, the more anguished he became and he wailed in great agony. Then he lay down on the living room floor behind my piano bench and seemed to go into a trance. His body stiffened and his arms stuck straight out at his sides as he lay on his back. Then, ceasing his crying, his whole body began to jerk convulsively and his face contorted, his arms and body remaining in the rigid shape of a cross.

I continued playing the three verses as I'd been told.

Amos looked pitiful and I felt sorry for him but I knew there was nothing we could do. Only wait and find out later what it meant.

I finally reached the end of the song and swung around on the bench. Amos relaxed and sat up slowly. Two tears trickled down his ruddy cheeks.

"What happened, Amos?" I asked.

In a husky voice, full of emotion, he answered, "I saw Jesus crucified on the cross. I saw the whole thing. I not only saw the whole thing, but I felt the nails being driven into his feet and into his hands. I felt the spear in my side—and I felt the crown of thorns—" He covered his face with his hands, still trembling. "I felt the awful pain of the spear as it was thrust into Jesus' side—"

The room fell silent for a moment, then one by one we all began dabbing at the tears in our eyes. Why we were given this graphic depiction of the suffering of Christ we didn't know, but it was awesome and humbling. For many years to come, whenever I was tempted to bemoan the hardships I had to endure, I'd be reminded of Amos—and how we'd seen through his body what Christ had suffered not for His sin, but for mine. My suffering could never compare with His.

There was one question I had to ask Amos. "Why do you think I had to play three verses of that song?"

"One for the Father, one for the Son and one for the Holy Spirit," he answered directly.

It was four o'clock when we finally retired to our bedrooms. I knew tomorrow (or rather today) was Sunday and I had to be at the church for Sunday school but I wasn't worried about being tired. Ron had said that the Lord was going to give me the equivalent of eight hours of sleep in the couple of hours I actually had.

When my alarm jarred me awake two hours later, I awoke refreshed.

After the Sunday morning service which proceeded normally, the young people wanted to stay to sing and pray. This was not customary, but I agreed, not particularly wanting to discourage their new-found enthusiasm. Not surprisingly, that service ended the way all our others had been doing lately. But there was one message given to me that was a little unsettling.

"Gerald, you shall not speak in tongues today, but you shall soon."

I had almost forgotten my silent prayer a few nights ago. Evidently God hadn't. Again, at least I wouldn't have to worry about it happening to me today. I really wasn't anxious for it any more.

My wife and I held the responsibility of overseeing a small Mennonite mission in downtown Fargo, North Dakota, one Sunday evening a month. This happened to be that day and we made preparations to go. Several of the teen-agers expressed an interest in accompanying us, so we piled them into our car.

I always looked forward to ministering in this little ghetto mission, sixty miles away. The "down-and-outers" who made up the audience always had so many needs and our being there seemed to help so much.

We hadn't gone far down the bumpy road when one of the teen-agers in the back seat began to prophesy. This was getting to be the norm now, so I just listened.

"Gerald, do you feel the bumps beneath the wheels of your automobile? As bumpy and rough as this road is to your car will be the experience you will have to go through before you speak in tongues and receive a new anointing in your ministry."

There it was again. God was not forgetting my prayer and now I almost wished I hadn't prayed it. What did he mean by a "rough and bumpy experience"? The dirt road we were on was extremely bad from the ice and snow. In fact, it was like a washboard, almost jarring the insides out of us. I guessed that meant that whatever I had to go through wasn't going to be pleasant.

Our meeting in Fargo turned out just like all the recent meetings. People fell over into trances, spoke in tongues, and prophesied. Many were saved and the Spirit of God fell on that little mission.

It was very late by the time we made it back home. But as we drove up the lane we noticed lights on in our house again. Sure enough, there were a few young people there. And strange things were happening. When I started to tell them what had happened in Fargo, they stopped me.

"We already know all that happened," one of the boys said. "Betty was lying on the floor the whole time you were gone and she's been telling us everything you've been doing."

"What?" I asked. "How did she do that?"

"From the time you left till now, God has been showing her everything; she saw and related to us every move you've made." He proceeded to tell us some of the things that had happened in Fargo. They were absolutely accurate in every detail! I couldn't believe my ears. This was like television—without the set!

Just then I heard someone's voice calling me from the living room. "Gerald, you, Beulah, Amos, Arnie (my associate pastor) and his wife are to be at the church Monday morning between six and eight o'clock. There will be two people to meet you there."

That was the message given me twice before. Now I

had no excuse but to follow directions. I just wished he'd set the time a little later. It was already one-thirty in the morning and we hadn't been getting much sleep.

"Gerald!" My name was being called again and I hurried over to the side of Skip who was lying on the couch, his eyes closed.

"Gerald, you shall likely speak in tongues before the night is over."

Oh, no. Not that again. I wouldn't have minded waiting till morning. Besides, it was late and I was tired.

"Are you going to wait up and see what happens?" Beulah asked. She had just put the children in their beds and was standing at my side.

"No, I'm tired; I'm going to bed," I answered. Anyway, God had said, "likely." That meant there was a chance He wasn't going to do it tonight after all.

With that last message, Amos, Freddy, Johnny, Joy and Beverly went upstairs to sleep and the other young people went home. Beulah and I sank wearily into our beds.

Little did I know that my "bumpy" experience was only hours away. It would be an introduction to a week during which we would be maneuvered like marionettes in a bizarre and supernatural play by a powerful force in the setting of our home.

11

The Fire Spreads

The next thing I remembered was a thunderous banging on the back door of our house. Someone was pounding on the wooden door so hard it shuddered and strained on its hinges.

I was awake in an instant. Beulah sat up in bed. "What's that? What's going on? Gerald, someone's trying to get in!"

I swung the covers off and my feet found the cold bare floor.

"Stay there. I'll go see who it is," I said firmly. Glancing at the alarm clock next to the bed, I noticed it was five-thirty in the morning. It was still pitch black outside.

I walked quickly to the door in my pj's. Whoever was out there seemed bent on pounding the door down. I switched on the light, turned the key in the lock, and gasped when I saw who was standing there—one of our neighbors, Mr. Carlton. He lived down the road, and although he and his wife were not Christians, his daughter, Beverly, was in our upstairs bedroom now. She was one of those who had been involved in some of the strange happenings that had been going on at the church lately. She was a lovely young girl who was sincerely dedicated to the Lord. She had been concerned for her parents. I knew them quite well from my Watkins route and had been in their home many times.

"Come in, Mr. Carlton," I said now. "What can I do for—"

"I have come to settle this thing *right now!*" he said. I was shocked to see he was boiling mad. His face was flushed and contorted into a snarl by anger.

"I'm sick and tired of all this religious nonsense!" he yelled. "I came here tonight to beat you all up—all of you! I want all the people in this house to come outside so I can beat 'em up. Right now!"

I stared at him in disbelief. I couldn't fathom why he would be so angry at us. He was literally quivering with rage as he clenched and unclenched his fists. Beat up my family? I just couldn't believe he was saying those words. He was my neighbor and there had never been a harsh remark between us.

"Why, Mr. Carlton—I love you!" I found myself saying. It just came out.

"Don't you tell me you love me, you good-for-nothing———! Ever since you young squirts have come to this community, all the people talk about is church, church, church! They've all gone crazy—a bunch of religious fanatics runnin' around." He was shouting even louder now and was waving his arms in the air and shaking his fist in my face. He glared at me, breathing heavily.

"I'm gonna stop this *right now!* Put an end to it. I want you all out in the back yard here and I'm gonna settle it once and for all!"

"B-b-but, Mr. Carlton, I *do* love you!" I said urgently. Again it was the only thing I could say.

Our eyes locked for an instant. Then Mr. Carlton stated flatly, "I'm goin' home!" And with that he did an about-face, slammed the door behind him, climbed in his car, and disappeared down the lane. Just like that.

All of a sudden I began to tremble with fear. I shook like a leaf in the wind. Then it occurred to me that I had been absolutely fearless all the while he'd been there threatening bodily harm to my family and myself. It was only after he'd gone that I began to tremble. Not a bad time to get frightened!

I looked out the window and as I watched the red taillights of Mr. Carlton's car disappear, a verse from the Bible came to me: "When the enemy shall come in like a flood, the Spirit of the Lord shall lift up a standard against him" (Isa. 59:19).

That's what had happened. God had raised up a protective wall around me and that angry man couldn't touch me. I had felt the air whoosh by my face as he swung his fists but he hadn't been able to touch me.

Because of our Mennonite beliefs in nonresistance I had always wondered what I would do in a situation like this—where not only my life was threatened, but the lives of my wife and babies. In fact, my friends would ask me," Gerald, what would you do if someone came to your house and tried to kill your wife? You mean you wouldn't try to stop them? Don't you keep a gun in the house, just in case?"

I never really knew what to say. If they pressed me I had to answer, "I guess I'd have to let the person commit the crime. At least my family would be ready to die while the murderer wouldn't. If I took his life I'd send him to hell." I hated to answer the question that way, but I didn't know of any other answer.

Now, after this morning, I knew what my answer to that question would be. "I'll wait till something happens, then I'll tell you what I did." I was convinced now that God honored my nonresistant convictions to the point that He would either prevent such a situation from ever arising, or He would fight the battle for me in His own way. What better weapon could there be?

I walked back to the bedroom.

"Who was that?" Beulah asked. "Wasn't it Mr. Carlton?"

"Yes, it was," I answered.

"What did he want?" she asked again. But before I could answer she said, "Gerald, call Amos."

For some reason I followed her instruction immediately without question. Amos was sleeping in one of our upstairs bedrooms, so I walked to the foot of the stairs right outside our bedroom door and called: "Amos!"

He answered at once. "Coming, Gerald." It was almost as if he'd been waiting to be called. He came directly down the steps, but as soon as he reached the first floor, he paused and called another name.

"Joy!"

Joy was staying in our other upstairs bedroom. She too answered in the same manner. "Coming!" It was like clockwork.

Amos walked into our moonlit bedroom and Joy came after him, both of them fully dressed. Then Joy began to speak in that unnatural way and I knew God had something in mind that was about to happen.

"Gerald, do you remember the prophecy which said that before you spoke in tongues you would have to go through a hard battle?"

I nodded. "Yes, I remember." So this was it!

"Gerald, this was not Mr. Carlton you were facing. That was his body you saw and his voice you heard, but Satan was in his body. Gerald, you showed your love to

116

Mr. Carlton. Therefore, reach out and take hold of my hand."

Joy was standing on the opposite side of the bed. Beulah still was in the bed and Amos stood next to Joy. I hesitated momentarily before taking her hand. It bothered me that she'd said I had shown *my* love to Mr. Carlton. It wasn't *my* love. I could never have loved that man in that condition. No way. It had to be a supernatural love—one that came straight from God. I couldn't take credit for it.

Nevertheless, I reached out in the semi-darkness and clasped Joy's hand.

The moment I touched her hand I burst forth like a mighty fountain that had just been unplugged—in a language I had never learned. It gushed uncontrollably from the depths of my being like a geyser. At first it seemed as if I were rebuking the devil. Then an overwhelming joy came over me and I literally trembled from head to foot out of sheer exuberance. The trembling was so intense that I nearly danced all over that bedroom. My tongue was going a mile a minute and all I could feel was unspeakable joy and gratitude, praise and love for Jesus. I never wanted to stop. This had to be heaven—forever and ever praising Him, enjoying a high that just kept increasing in intensity!

But after I had gone on in this manner for a time, I dimly heard Amos's voice commanding me to stop.

"Gerald, stop! In the name of Jesus, stop!"

How could he do this to me? I didn't want to stop and furthermore, I didn't think I could if I wanted to. With great effort, however, I obeyed and finally got my body and tongue under control.

Then Amos interpreted in English all that I had said in

tongues. And as soon as his interpretation was finished, he and Joy left the room and climbed the stairs back to their bedrooms. The first hint of dawn had diluted the darkness when I crawled back into bed, still feeling like I was in another world.

Now that Beulah and I were baptized in the Holy Spirit, God was able to continue this week which would so radically change our lives. There was no trace of doubt now in my mind as to God's hand in all of this. Still, at that time, I had no conception of what we would experience before the week was over.

After several minutes had passed, I remembered what day it was—Monday. It was 5:50 now and we had to be at the church by six. We both got up and began to get dressed.

"What about the children?" Beulah asked. "I really don't think we should get them up and take them along at this hour."

"H'm. I don't know," I replied. Both of them were in our room and had slept through all the commotion of my speaking in tongues. I breathed a prayer, asking God what He wanted us to do about the children.

Just then Joanne turned over on her pallet on the floor at the foot of our bed and heaved a sigh. Along with that sigh, her lips formed a word: "Amos."

"Did you hear what she said?" Beulah asked, stepping over and looking down at the little girl under the mound of blankets. She was still sound asleep.

"Yes. Didn't she say, 'Amos'?"

"Uh-huh. Maybe Amos knows what we're supposed to do with the children. Call him," Beulah answered.

I mounted the stairs marveling at how God had spoken through a three-year-old child. Amos did have the answer to our problem. He stated without hesitation that Beverly was to stay with them.

When Beulah, Amos, and I arrived at the church, my associate pastor and his wife were already there, just as the Lord had said earlier. Amos began giving orders.

First of all, he told us we were to expect a visit from Mr. Carlton and his wife. "You are not to fear," he told us. "We will be engaging in a spiritual battle and we are to be like soldiers, courageous and brave. There is to be no fear." It was a command.

Then he told us to line up in front of the pulpit, facing the front door of the church. It was very apparent that Amos was not his usual self and that we were being given orders from a higher power, so we quickly obeyed.

"Do not fear," he repeated. "Now let us sing with all our might 'Victory in Jesus.' Then we are to sing 'Power in the Blood.' "

We proceeded to do as he said and when we finished we remained standing there. In those few moments of time, Beulah had a vision of the Crucifixion of Jesus and she cried as she described it to us.

"Now Mr. Carlton and his wife are on their way here," Amos spoke up again. "They will be very angry because Satan has entered their bodies. But remember, do not fear, God will give us the victory. This will be a hard battle, but we must have faith. Do not doubt."

Amos walked toward us down the aisle and pointed to the floor a few feet in front of us.

"This is the blood line. If we have no doubts among us, Mr. and Mrs. Carlton will not be able to cross this line. And if we fervently trust and believe, they will have a true deliverance right here."

About this time I found myself struggling against

terrible doubts. I don't know about the others, but my spirit was fighting a losing battle with my mind. It seemed the more I tried to have faith and believe, the harder it became. It was like someone taking your picture with a flash camera and telling you not to blink. My brain kept telling me we were all acting foolish and how long would we have to stand here if no one showed up?

We started singing again. Then Amos said, "Now let's stand straight, hands to our sides and look neither to the right nor left. They are now rounding the corner at the grocery store and will be here very soon."

We straightened our line and waited, standing at attention. The grocery store was only a mile down the road. I strained my ears. Was that the sound of a car? My pulse began to quicken and I resisted the urge to glance at Beulah. Sure enough. The sound was getting closer. Then we saw headlights outside the church windows and my chest began to pound. The car turned into the parking lot and we heard a car door slam.

What a sight we must have been, the five of us lined up in front of the pulpit like the military. We stood silently now in the dim light. I shoved the fear down inside of me as I desperately tried to comply with our strict instructions.

The front door jerked open and Mrs. Carlton stepped in. Her hair was disheveled and her cheeks and nose were red from the cold. She glared at us and demanded, "Where's Beverly?" Her voice echoed loudly through the small frame building.

No one answered. We stood staring at her.

She walked about halfway down the aisle, her boots leaving little clumps of snow in her tracks. "Where is my daughter? I want to know!"

We stood there stone-faced.

Now she came up to the blood line and peered into our faces. "Will somebody answer me? Where is Beverly?"

For some reason none of us was able to speak. All we could do was stare at her. And try not to doubt.

But now she was really mad. She began yelling and calling us names. "I'm gonna get my husband," she finally said in exasperation. "He'll get some answers out of you!" She turned on her heel and ran out the door.

Presently Mr. Carlton was confronting us. It wasn't much more than an hour since I'd seen him, but somehow it seemed like days.

"*Where's Beverly!*" he roared from where he stood at the door. "I'll make you talk, you bunch of dummies!"

He clomped noisily up the aisle to the blood line, then *across* the line and right up to our faces. I was petrified. I couldn't believe what was happening.

Mr. Carlton ranted and raved, demanding to know where his daughter was. His fists swung heavily in front of our noses.

Just then my voice erupted into tongues. And as soon as I started, the others joined me. We all stood in a straight line and spoke in tongues at Mr. Carlton. It was more than he could take. He bolted for the door, hurling insults and curses over his shoulder. He kicked open the maple wood church door. It slammed against the guard rail outside and splintered, leaving a long crack that remained for many years to come.

As soon as they were gone, Amos began to talk.

"Mr. and Mrs. Carlton are now going down the road towards your house, Gerald. Now they are turning into the driveway. Mrs. Carlton is getting out of the car and going into your house—"

I looked over at Beulah and our eyes met. I knew she was thinking the same thing I was. The children. And Beverly, the Carlton's teen-age daughter, was supposed to be taking care of them.

Dear God, I breathed, protect our babies.

Beverly, a mature, brown-haired, eighteen-year-old with a sweet, round face, had grown up in this neck of the woods and was totally capable of taking care of our little ones. She was one of my first converts and even wore the plain Mennonite clothing. I shuddered now as I thought of what her parents would do in their irrational state upon finding her at our house.

Amos continued on. "Mrs. Carlton has gone into the kitchen. She sees Beverly and is screaming at her. Now she has grabbed her by the covering and by the hair and is slapping her face. But Beverly's spirit has left her body and she is with Jesus. Her body has gone limp and her mother and father are dragging her out of the house and lifting her into the car." Amos paused, then said, "They are starting the car now and are going home."

He fell silent and moments later, the Carlton's car passed by the church.

"We may go home now," Amos said.

Dawn had broken outside and I knew Beulah was having a very hard time staying calm through Amos's narration. Surely the children had seen and heard all that had happened—if indeed it had happened. We were sure Ron and Joy were still at the house, but they were sound asleep as far as we knew and the children would be alone if Beverly wasn't there.

Moments later when we walked into the house, Joanne came running up to Beulah.

"Mommy, mommy! They hit Beb'rly and pulled her by da hair!" she said tearfully.

"That's okay, honey," Beulah soothed, scooping the little girl up in her arms and pressing her face onto her shoulder.

"They took her 'way, a bad man and lady—" she continued as Beulah took her into the bedroom.

Joy was awake by now, but Ron slept until noon. And when he awoke he had quite a story to tell.

"Did you just wake up, Ron?" I asked, wondering how he could have slept through all the commotion.

"Yeah, and you won't believe the dream I just had," he answered.

"What do you mean?" I said, almost afraid to ask.

"It was so real. I saw some people that looked really angry come into the kitchen here and slap Beverly and drag her out the door. In fact, I think it was her parents. Anyway, the funny thing was it seemed her spirit left her body. That's the best I can explain it anyway, and she was with Jesus and couldn't feel anything happening to her. It was really strange." He stopped now and looked around. "Hey, where is Beverly anyway?"

I took a deep breath. "Ron, what you dreamed was probably exactly what happened here a few hours ago." Quickly I briefed him in on all we'd seen and heard since early that morning.

Later that day Beverly came back to our house and verified all that had happened, exactly as God had revealed it to us. It seems when she came to, her parents couldn't look her in the face for the bright light that shone there. They threw her out of the house and she hitchhiked back to our place.

"But I didn't feel anything," she exclaimed. "I felt like I

was with Jesus and I was just looking down and observing all that was taking place with my body. I saw mom and dad carry my body to the car, but I was having a beautiful time."

The fires of revival licked at our home for the next six days. We lived a totally abnormal life. Our activities were not scheduled by the clock. Through the lips of one of the dozen or so people who were in and out of the house during that time, God instructed us precisely what to do and how to do it every minute of the day. He told us when to pray, when to sing, when to cry, when to rejoice, and with what intensity to do it. We were told who was en route to our home, how far away they were, and why they were coming. Even our mealtimes and bedtimes were regulated. We were told when we could eat, what we should eat, who was to do the dishes, when we could sleep, who could sleep, and for how long. Everyone slept in their clothes.

Our young children, awed into silence for the whole time, also fit into the mosaic of happenings, and were used by God specifically in several instances.

Not only did God let us see Him in an unusual way, but He allowed Satan to reveal himself. Our experiences ranged from the gloriously ecstatic to the hideously demonic. Yet God was always totally in control and everything was in perfect order. He pulled the switches and gave the cues.

Everything had to be perfect during this time—perfect like human beings are not. No unnecessary words were allowed. Exclamations such as, "Oh, my goodness!", "Dear me!", or "Goodness gracious!" and the like were sternly rebuked by the words, "Let your yea be yea and your nay be nay."

Any mistake or disobedience did not go unpunished. We learned explicitly what the fear of God was.

One of the greatest things we had to deal with was doubt. We were instructed not to doubt, but many times our human frailness precluded our being able to follow this in its purest form. God made known every thought that crossed our minds and when someone began to doubt, others were instructed to lay hands on that person and pray he would believe. Many times I would have a specific question on my mind and before I could even verbalize it, the Lord spoke through someone with the answer.

It was so perfect and so strange that if I'd known ahead of time what was going to happen, I'd have driven 5,000 miles away from that place. On the other hand it was so glorious that if heaven is anything like that was, it is worth it all.

As far as we knew, we would live like this for the rest of our lives. We were not told how long it would last. We had no control over its beginning and we knew of no way to stop it.

12

Battling With Satan

And as he was yet a coming, the devil threw him
down, and tare him. And Jesus rebuked the
unclean spirit, and healed the child, and
delivered him again to his father. (Luke 9:42)

I never thought much about the devil before. My con-
cept of him was like almost everyone's, I guess. A big,
ugly, black monster with glowing coals for eyes, having
horns and a forked tail and holding a pitchfork. He was
some undefinable spirit that temporarily had control of
the world, according to the Bible, until Christ's return
when all the powers of evil would be banished forever.

During our visitation experience from God, however,
we were brought face to face with Satan. To the same
degree that God revealed himself to us, so was the devil
revealed. Our human minds and bodies were pushed to
the limit, so much so that after the revival had ended we
were told we looked like dishrags, so wrung out. It was a
basic training in spiritual warfare that I was grateful
for many times over in the years that followed.

Confronting the devil as we had to do at various times
was a shocking, chilling and dramatic experience. And
always a point was made perfectly clear. Satan is no
match for God and His people. After every wrenching

battle there was victory and the victories were just as thrilling as the battles were tough.

When these encounters occurred it was my duty to stand guard at our door since I was the head of the house. This was necessary because when Satan entered someone's body we could not predict what would happen and sometimes the person would try to run out the door. He would invariably crash to the floor writhing and struggling with an invisible "person." Strange noises would come out of his mouth and his face would contort with ugly grimaces. We were told to gather around and pray fervently at these times, to rebuke the devil and command him to leave the person alone. Sometimes Satan would speak through the person's mouth in an unnatural masculine voice, mocking and ridiculing us or the person he possessed. When we prayed with all our might, the devil would finally leave, although on several instances he planted himself in someone else in the room. Then we'd have to start rebuking all over again.

For reasons unknown to us, Amos was used by God and Satan more than anyone else. He was born and raised in the Amish faith, which is even more plain and conservative than the Mennonites. His parents adhered to the traditional clothing and way of life—long dresses of coarse, dark fabric, white opaque prayer veilings covered by black bonnets for the women. The men wore black homespun suits and wide-brimmed hats as well as full beards. A horse and buggy provided transportation and they lived in farmhouses with no electricity or modern conveniences. Even the farming equipment was forbidden to have rubber tires. Steel-rimmed wheels were tolerated.

Although they believe in the Bible, these people are not

taught salvation through the blood of Jesus. They attempt to live a good, moral, religious life, separate from the world, and hope that when they die God will see fit to let them into heaven. They speak the German dialect and send their children to their own schools. The Amish, even moreso than the Mennonites, are very clannish and stay to themselves. In modern times it has become increasingly difficult for them to retain their way of life and their numbers have dwindled considerably. Although they are a peace-loving people, they practice "shunning," which means that if community or family members stray from the Amish faith, they are ignored or cut off from the family; in other words, they are shunned.

A tall, good-looking boy, Amos had thick, dark hair with a distinguishing feature—a white streak that ran from his forehead to his crown. He had an outgoing, gregarious personality that made him a favorite among the young people. We first met Amos on one of his regular truck-driving trips to deliver canned goods to our mission. His yen for adventure combined with a considerable amount of wanderlust made him unusual for an Amishman back then, and it remained with him as long as we've known him. Always full of exciting stories, he had a built-in knack for telling them.

Yet Amos had a very simple, childlike quality about him. And looking back, I wonder if that's why God singled him out for so many of the dramatic experiences we had to go through during that revival.

When Amos left our place to go home after the visitation he was not allowed to eat at the same table with his family. Although they did let him in as one of the family, he was required to sit at a separate table when eating.

The second morning of that memorable week in our home, Amos came downstairs to the breakfast table where Beulah and I sat eating.

"Gerald," he said, "the Holy Spirit just told me that Satan was out to kill me."

I looked up at him in surprise. "What?"

"Satan's out to kill me, but God said He wouldn't let it happen if you are all faithful in what you are to do," he finished quietly.

I set my coffee cup down on the table, got up and put my hands on his shoulders.

"Don't worry, Amos. We'll be faithful. With God's help, we'll be faithful."

"Yes, that's right," Beulah added. "Maybe we all ought to pray for Amos now, Gerald."

"Yes, let's do that," I answered, getting down on my knees. I called Freddy, Johnny, Joy, and the others in the house and we all laid hands on Amos and prayed that God would strengthen him and help us all to be faithful for whatever might be ahead.

A few moments later it became evident that Amos was going to be used as an example for us. God was going to require absolute perfection from him as a prerequisite. And the first step in this purification process was a strange one. We were told to burn all his clothes!

Joy spoke up. "Amos, you are to go into the bedroom and undress. Freddy and Johnny, you go get a pail of water, a scrub brush and soap and scrub him down thoroughly."

They all did exactly as they were told.

"Now take all of Amos's clothes, along with his shoes and wallet with everything in it, to the furnace and burn them." These were our next instructions.

The boys obediently went downstairs to the collar where a fire roared in the furnace. They opened the grate and threw the clothes in. From where I stood at the top of the stairs I heard one of the boys yell, "Hey, look at that!"

"What's happening?" I asked quickly.

"They're not burning! The clothes are lying in the fire but they're not burning!" Freddy exclaimed.

Several more minutes passed. Then we heard a muffled explosion.

"There they go! Did you hear that? They're all gone now," Johnny called. The clothes had disintegrated in a burst of brilliant blue flames. The boys scrambled up the stairs and we all wondered what would happen next.

That afternoon, Joy and Louise's mother, Marabel, came to the house. She was a new Christian and quite apprehensive about what was going on, especially since part of her family was involved. I left them alone to talk in the living room and walked to the kitchen.

Amos, dressed in a clean change of clothes, was sitting at the table talking in tongues. Although he was alone, it seemed as if he was having a conversation with someone. Beulah and I and Beverly stood and watched him until finally he turned to us and said, "I just had a talk with Satan. He claims he has permission from God to wrestle with me." He paused and we looked at each other in mute silence.

"I must be faithful and go through with this. If I don't, he says he has permission to take it out on anyone else in this room." He stopped momentarily, then said simply, "Pray."

He got up, walked through the kitchen and into the enclosed small porch and shut the door behind him. Then we heard a crunching thud that sounded like he had fallen to the floor. Almost immediately the sounds of a knock-down, drag-out fight met our ears. With all the kicking and thrashing around it seemed incredible that there was only one man in that room. We became sickeningly aware that the other "person" that wrestled with Amos was the devil. He cried out in pain, then gasped as if the air had been knocked out of him.

I grabbed the hands of those standing around me and said, "Let's pray!" We started pleading for the protection of the blood of Jesus.

All of a sudden the kitchen door flew open and Amos's body rolled into the room, still writhing violently. He was in agony. At times he would make short jabs into the air with his fists as if hitting someone or his mouth would open and his head fall back and he'd gasp for air as if someone were choking him. He was obviously fighting for his life. All we could do was pray harder and try not to let fear overwhelm us. And it was a fearful sight—this strapping young man grappling on the floor with every ounce of his strength against a power that almost seemed to be getting the best of him. We were utterly helpless against it.

Finally, with the sweat pouring off his face, we heard him say a word. It seemed to be a name. He forced it out with a gasp.

"Mar-a-bel!"

As if on cue, Marabel, who had been in the living room with her daughters, marched into the kitchen like a trooper. Looking neither to the right nor left, she walked up to Amos, slapped her hand on his forehead and commanded, *"In Jesus' name!"*

Amos's body immediately went limp and he fell back relaxed. The muscles in his face smoothed out and he lay there motionless. The battle was over.

Marabel then grasped his right hand and began to give a powerful dissertation. I couldn't believe my eyes. This woman was barely a Christian and she hadn't even been in on any of this revival in our home up to now. Surely she had never heard anyone prophesy or speak in tongues. She was a housewife and mother of seven children. But now she was speaking like a veteran prophetess.

"Amos, because you have been faithful in your battle with Satan, the Lord says to you that you will never have to go through a battle like this again. The Lord is pleased with your faithfulness and He will bless you and reward you accordingly."

With that, Marabel took her hand from Amos, turned to me and said, "Gerald, I understand now what is happening here. It is from the Lord. Joy and Louise are to stay here until the Lord says they can go." Her maternal misgivings were quieted by the Spirit and she no longer worried about her daughters.

Another time Satan was out to kill *me*. Several of us were given detailed instructions on how to hold Amos's body down when the murderous spirit entered. I was to wrap my arms tightly around his legs and two others were to secure his arms as he lay on the couch. During the five minutes or so during the battle, one of his arms got loose and flailed the air, barely missing my face. I held on with all my might to his legs and just when it seemed I could hang on no longer one of the other boys in the room came over, slapped his hand on Amos's forehead and shouted, "In the name of Jesus, *come out!*"

Amos's body relaxed. When he came to, he told us that all he could remember was that he was bent on killing me. My chest and arms were stiff for many days after that.

During one of the beginning days of that week, God spoke through one of the young people telling us there would be a line of blood encircling our house extending forty feet, through which Satan could not enter. Only through God's specific permission could the devil or anyone else penetrate this blood line.

However, our outside bathroom facilities and also the doghouse were beyond that limit. So whenever someone had to go to the outhouse or anywhere near the doghouse, the rest of us had to join hands and sing songs of victory until they returned. I would usually be stationed at the door.

The full impact of this situation was made very real to us one time when we stopped singing before Amos had gotten past this line and into the house. To our horror, Sporty, our big black Labrador, who was always extremely gentle and friendly, leaped up and clamped his teeth on Amos's throat.

Freddy, who happened to be guarding the door at that time, began screaming, "Sing! Sing!"

"O victory in Jesus, my Savior forever! . . ." I immediately began.

Amos stumbled into the door, his neck still wet with the dog's saliva. We embraced his trembling body.

Freddy was talking excitedly. "I really saw Satan enter that dog! Then when you started singing again, he left, and the dog let go. Wow!" He shook his head in amazement.

"You okay, Amos?" I asked.

He rubbed his neck. "Yeah. I'm all right."

I looked out the kitchen window. Sporty was standing there looking up at me, wagging his tail. As always.

Someone had started singing again when I walked back

into the living room. So I sat down at the piano and began to play. After what we'd gone through it was only natural to want to praise the Lord. One of the instructions we were repeatedly given was when we did something unto the Lord, whether it be rejoicing or travailing, we were to do it with *all* our might. Not halfheartedly, but with everything we could muster. This usually turned out to be an easy order, for the encounters we had were so intense we needed no prompting to follow them up properly.

On the other hand, it was still hard for me to be entirely spontaneous with my praise. Others seemed to shed their inhibitions much more readily than I. And I envied them for it. But as time progressed, little by little I began to care less and less about what anyone would think of me and was able to join with them.

And what a sight we made! We'd start out singing for a while, then begin raising our hands. We would lift our faces to the ceiling, and make our own tune as we sang praises to our Lord and Savior. Then someone would start shouting. "Hallelujah" and "Praise the Lord" reverberated off the walls of that little house in the woods. It was deafening at times.

Other times there would be dancing. Those proper, demure young Mennonite ladies in their cape dresses and prayer coverings would tiptoe around the room, into the kitchen, and back to the living room again, their hands and faces lifted heavenward. The men, too, joined in. Their eyes would be closed and their glowing faces radiated a joy that could not be described. Our two babies would be playing on the floor in the midst of all this and amazingly would never get stepped on. Six or seven people would glide around them gracefully as if some great choreographer had meticulously planned the production. At those times it seemed as if heaven itself had settled over our little home. We'd lose all track of time, never tiring until God brought something else onto the agenda.

"Dancing in the Spirit" was something very far removed from what Mennonites would have done normally. We had been strictly taught against dancing in any way, shape or form. We were not to dance anywhere—and certainly not in church! But now we were being led by something more than what we'd been taught in church. It was pure, innocent, holy and pleasing to God. He told us it was.

Since I was usually told to play the piano, I probably danced less than the others, but Beulah was one of the regulars. She displayed a childlike abandonment that made me well up with joy as I watched her float gracefully around the room on her tiptoes. It was a taste of freedom we had never known—freedom from generations of deeply ingrained inhibitions and fear of reproach, a freedom that was guilt-free because of its sole purpose, that of giving unrestrained adoration to God, our Father.

The battles were always worth the victory celebrations. It was during one of these celebrations that the first hole was punched in our ceiling.

13

Holes in the Ceiling

We were all in the living room and had just finished praying over someone's need. Now we were rejoicing, doing it with all our might as we were required.

All at once Amos leaped into the air, threw his arms up, shouted, "Hallelujah," and sank a fist right through our low, soft Celotex-board ceiling! White chalky chunks of debris dropped to the floor. Startled for an instant, Amos looked up in disbelief at what he'd done. The room grew silent.

Then before anyone had time to react, Amos went into a semi-trance and said, "Gerald, what do you think of this?"

I looked up at the gaping hole. We could have it fixed. It was a low ceiling and I guessed it would have happened with any tall man like Amos. Although it surely seemed odd, accidents happened and this wasn't that drastic.

"We can have it fixed," I answered. "It's all right."

"Gerald, what would you think if this happened again?" Amos countered.

Thinking it would be some coincidence for it to happen again, I answered, "If it happened again I guess it would be all right too. We could have it repaired."

"What would you think if there were many holes punched in your ceiling?" Amos asked again.

"Many holes?" Now this was really sounding strange. I thought for a moment, then replied. "This is the Lord's house, and if it is His will that there are many holes punched in our ceiling then it would be all right."

"Freddy," Amos said after that, "go get Joanne's box of crayons in the lower drawer on the right side of the desk in the bedroom."

Freddy did as he was told, bringing Joanne and her box of Crayolas into the living room.

"Now step onto a chair and with a red crayon trace around the jagged edges of the hole."

Beulah picked up a kitchen chair brought it into the living room, and set it under the hole. She stepped back next to me and whispered, "Gerald, what is going on?"

"Sh-h-h-h, I'm not really sure. We just have to do as we're told," I assured her. Beulah's lips parted slightly as she stared silently along with the rest of us at the ceiling.

Freddy took the crayon Joanne handed up to him and proceeded to draw a border around the hole. When he was finished, Amos continued on.

"Now take the green crayon and print around the hole the request you prayed for."

Freddy followed suit, bracing his left hand on the ceiling while he carefully printed with the other. Then Amos explained, "This is to be a reminder that God has heard your prayers and what you have asked for will surely come to pass."

Before the week was over, there were twelve holes decorating our living room ceiling. Each one was out-lined with brightly colored lettering and each one represented a victory. Needless to say, our ceiling was a shocker to anyone coming into the house for the first time.

Although we were taken by surprise every time someone's fist punctuated the ceiling, we grew accustomed to the occurrence and accepted it as the Lord's doing. In the midst of all the bizarre things that were going on, the holes just seemed to fit in. Sometimes in the middle of the night, while Beulah and I lay in bed, we'd hear a shout—then a hollow thunk followed by the muted sound of debris falling as someone's feet pounded back onto the floor.

Amos was the first one who had been given the ability to "see" people coming to and from our house while many miles away. He could also see Jesus and His angels and Satan and his demons at all times. It was a tremendous responsibility. Perhaps that was why God allowed another man to come onto the scene to share the burden.

Very early Tuesday morning I awakened with a start. It was still dark. Beulah was still sleeping. Just then I heard a car door slam. Footsteps crunched through the snow up to the door then stopped.

Knock, knock, knock.

I was already out of bed, pulling my trousers on. I snapped the porch light on, opened the door and stared into the face of Brother William, one of our Sunday school teachers at the church.

"Well, good morning, William," I said. "What can I do for you?"

His eyes fixed on me strangely and then he said in an authoritative voice, "I have come to give a message to Amos."

This wasn't the Brother William I knew. A smallish man with a slight build and nondescript face, he was a shy, retiring sort of fellow, the kind who rarely spoke unless spoken to.

Without waiting for my answer, he brushed by me stiffly, with his head up high and a determined look on his face. I followed him into the living room where Amos was already waiting. William marched up to Amos and grabbed his hand.

"You will no longer bear all the responsibility of God's anointing, but will share it with me. God awakened me and spoke these words and told me to give you this message."

Amos broke into a smile and raised his hands.

"Thank you, Jesus," he whispered.

They relaxed then and William explained what had happened. That night he'd had a vision of Jesus who told him to come to our house and give this message to Amos. At that time he had no idea what it meant, but it wasn't long before he found himself at our door.

So William and Amos were our "T.V. sets" of the spiritual world. They were automatically tuned in to whatever channel God wanted us to see. One or the other or both were at our house at all times. God's system of communication is infinitely more sophisticated than we can comprehend.

It was about six o'clock the next evening when William slumped over on the sofa and began telling us we were about to have a visitor.

"In a few moments a sheriff's deputy will be pulling into your driveway, Gerald."

I stepped over to the sofa and listened to what he was saying.

"Did you say the police are coming here?" I asked.

"Yes, but do not worry. The Lord will tell you what to say. Now everyone in the room form a circle, hold hands, and sing 'Victory in Jesus.' Gerald, you go to the door and wait for the deputy to arrive." He stopped while we carried out our orders. I looked out the window. Not a car in sight. The people in the living room started to sing. They sang loud and with gusto. They had to, for we were reminded repeatedly that we must do all we did with all our might. No halfhearted efforts, else we would be rebuked or punished. It always had to be our very best.

I grasped the doorknob and waited, looking out the kitchen window to see if I could catch a glimpse of anything. Sure enough, a car was approaching and pulling into the driveway. A police car. I was relieved to see that at least the red light wasn't flashing.

I waited for a moment, then stepped out onto the porch, down the steps, and over to the car. The deputy turned off his motor and stepped cautiously out of the car.

"Hello, sir," I stuck out my hand and forced a smile.

The man seemed as uncomfortable as I was. He shifted his feet nervously and his eyes avoided mine as he took my hand briefly. His silver badge glinted in the moonlight.

"Rev. Derstine, I'm sorry to bother you, but there have been some rumors going around about some strange things happening here—" He paused and finally met my gaze. The exuberant sounds of 'Victory in Jesus' wafted through the air. I got the feeling he felt like he was interrupting a church service.

"Oh, it's all right," I answered. "There are some strange things happening here, yes, but God is in charge and He has everything under control."

The policeman glanced at me again, caught my smile, then quickly fastened his attention to the tip of his boots.

"Well, Reverend, people have been calling me up, insisting that there's trouble here. They say your lights are on all night. There are people coming and going, and they even say you're getting hurt and your furniture's being smashed—" his voice trailed off again.

"Oh, no," I assured him. "We have had quite a few visitors lately but they're all very friendly and as you can tell by the singing, they're all very happy. We're fine. You have nothing to worry about."

"Well-l-l, I always thought you folks were a quiet, peace-loving kind and we've never had any trouble with you before. It's just that the community people insisted we come check it out. You understand, Reverend. If you don't mind, I would like to have the names of your out-of-state guests though."

"Surely," I answered. His fingers trembled as he wrote the names on his pad.

"Sorry to bother you. I'll go now and if we have any more complaints I'll just tell them everything's all right."

He was very anxious to leave.

"Don't worry about us," I said again as he turned and walked briskly back to his car. "God has everything under control."

The car sped off. I stamped the snow off my shoes and walked back into the warm house. Beulah met me at the door.

"Is everything all right?" she asked, touching my arm lightly.

"Just fine," I answered. "Everything's just fine."

"There Shall Be Revival!"

It was still late afternoon but it was already pitch black outside. There were no clouds and it was too cold to snow. Our guests were scattered throughout the living room and kitchen, talking quietly among themselves. Except for Amos, who was lying on the sofa with his eyes closed as though he were sleeping. Our trusty little furnace in the basement was performing admirably, sending blasts of heat through the vents bordering the floor.

Beulah, who was sitting across the room, caught my eye and motioned with her head towards Amos. When I looked at him I knew something was about to happen. He had started to tremble.

All at once he bolted off the sofa, marched into the kitchen and stood rigidly, his feet together, in the middle of the kitchen floor. His right hand shot straight up over his head and his left hand stiffened out perpendicular to his body. By this time he was trembling even more violently, in fact so much that his entire body vibrated up and down off the floor. Amos was a big man and with his frame bouncing flat-footed in that manner it caused the whole house to literally quake.

Now his mouth opened and his voice began to speak one word at a time, but with an unhuman, thunderous quality. It boomed out: "The sword of the Spirit is the

Word of the Lord! There shall be revival taking place on this earth like man has never witnessed in the history of the world—even greater than what took place on the day of Pentecost!"

We were spellbound. Not only was it an awesome sight to behold but the words which were roaring out with such great force were puzzling to us. As Mennonites we had always been taught that in the last days perilous times would come and there would be a great apostasy—a falling away. Now God was telling us repeatedly, in no uncertain terms, that a great revival was coming. Amos went on:

"No man nor any organization will receive any of the glory in this revival, but only the Lord thy God! He could have used a mule or an animal to bring this revival, but since He made man in His own likeness and image, He shall use man!"

These were the same words He had spoken through my own voice to the ministers in Detroit Lakes. God was confirming His Word. Amos's face had turned red and beads of sweat stood out on his forehead as he continued:

"This revival has thus far gone only as far as one and one-half drops in a ten-quart pail in comparison to what shall take place on this earth." He paused momentarily and then concluded, "This is not Amos speaking to you. This is Amos's body you see and Amos's voice you hear, but this is from the Lord your God!"

With that, his hands came down, his body stopped vibrating and he collapsed wearily into a chair with his head in his hands. All of us who had been watching were trembling now as we realized we had been in the presence of almighty God. As a body, we knelt on the floor and began thanking and praising God. With tears of unworthiness we worshiped this Being who had so honored us by His presence.

Even in the midst of such phenomena there were those of us who would deny the experience. There was one in particular among us who vacillated. One day he would come to the house and be a participant in the goings-on and the next day he would be out in the community telling people that what was going on was of Satan. He couldn't make up his mind. I was puzzled and a little fearful for him. I couldn't understand how that even after he'd received the "tongues experience" like the rest of us, he was turning his back on it.

We were to find out that God would not take it lightly. After the man finally left for good, God spoke in the usual way through one of the brethren. He came right to the point and spared no words: "Mr. ——— has blasphemed God." Perfect justice can be a terrible thing.

It was customary for me to go to Detroit Lakes every Wednesday morning to teach a class of high-schoolers at one of the local evangelical churches. The town's high school permitted any students who wished to spend their first-period class in the church for a Bible study.

I was one of five pastors who participated in this program. Besides myself, there were two Evangelical Free pastors, one Baptist, one Nazarene and one Assembly of God pastor. We would all share in these Wednesday morning classes, then meet together afterwards for a time of prayer. I was the youngest of the five.

It was Wednesday and unless I was told otherwise, I planned to go as usual. A glance at the clock told me it was time to get up and get ready if I was going to make it to town in time. I dressed and walked into the living room.

Several of my guests were already up.

Amos walked over to me. "Gerald," he said in a commanding voice. "You shall not go now."

Puzzled, I said, "But I'll be late if I don't go now."

"You will be there in time for what you are supposed to accomplish," he answered.

Quickly I took an assessment of the situation. By this time I knew I had to obey the Lord and stay until He said to go. There was no question as to that. In that case I would have to trust Him to help the other ministers understand my absence. I joined the others in the living room and we had a time of prayer and singing.

Forty-five minutes later, Amos spoke again.

"Gerald, you may go now."

Knowing I would be too late for the class, I prepared to go anyway. At least I would get there in time for the prayer fellowship with the other ministers. Besides, I thought I might get a chance to tell them what was going on at our house for the past few days.

But before I could step out the door, the Lord spoke again. *Gerald, when you go you must not speak of the things which have been happening in your home, for the ministers may not understand. They may think you are crazy or may consider this a work of the devil, thereby blaspheming the Holy Ghost. Do you understand?*

"Yes, I understand," I answered meekly.

That same message was repeated two more times. I understood perfectly.

Then a final message came. *Gerald, you shall do and act as you would have done and acted one month before any of these things ever took place in your home. Do you understand?*

"Yes, I understand," I replied.

That same message was also repeated two more times. For some reason, when God ever wanted to tell us something of extra importance, He would tell us three times. Whenever we were instructed to sing a certain song, we would be told to sing three verses. Or we would be told to do things in groups of three. When we asked the Lord about this, He would always say, "One for the Father, one for the Son, and one for the Holy Ghost." Numbers seemed to have special significance.

In a way I was relieved I didn't have to talk about our experiences to my minister friends. After all, if they began to really question me I might not know all the answers. There were so many things I myself did not understand.

I kissed Beulah good-bye, got in my car, and began the twenty-three-mile drive to Detroit Lakes. The morning was squeaky clean and the sun shone blindingly on the snow. I began to sing as I marveled at the exquisite loveliness of God's world. With all the trees stripped of their leaves it was easy to see far into the woods and perhaps catch the movement of a graceful buck or even the slinky flash of a coyote or wolf. Everything was so utterly still. The sturdy evergreens, the undersides of their succulent boughs peeking from coverlets of winter white, offered the only contrast in color from this dazzling world of white. I drove on, matching my tires to the tracks made in the snow by some other vehicle. Other than those tracks it was impossible to tell where the dirt road began and ended on either side.

Seven miles outside of town as my car topped a hill I felt a distinct sensation come over me. It started at the crown of my head and inched very slowly down my shoulders, arms, hips, and legs, ending at my toes like a warm blanket of oil. Although I was acutely aware of what was happening, I continued driving and once again reminded myself of what I'd been instructed by the Lord before I left. I was telling absolutely nothing to anyone about what had been happening.

Upon reaching my destination at the Evangelical Free church, I noticed the last of the students leaving. I grabbed my Bible and let myself into the front door.

"Good morning, Brother Derstine!" the host pastor exclaimed, waving a hand in greeting.

I threw my hand up to acknowledge his greeting but for some reason when I did so it froze there like a salute. I couldn't move or talk.

Shock registered on the pastor's face. "Gerald, did you see God?" he blurted.

The Baptist pastor was right behind him. "Were you praying all night?"

"Is your church having a revival meeting just now?" a third one asked anxiously.

I remained standing, stiff as a palace guard, my arm raised in a salute. Then I began speaking, slowly, forcefully, one word at a time, staring straight ahead.

"The Lord has spoken and said there shall be a revival coming upon this earth like man has never witnessed in the history of the world—even greater than that which took place on the day of Pentecost. In this revival, no man nor any organization shall receive any of the glory but only the *Lord thy God!*"

I continued, "The Lord could have used a mule or other animal to bring this revival to pass, but since He has made man after His own image and in His own likeness, He shall use man.

"This revival has thus far gone only as far as one and

one-half drops in a ten-quart pail in comparison with what shall take place on this earth!"

My hand now moved upward and moved in a semicircle, encompassing the four pastors as they stood watching me.

"Brethren, *pray like you've never prayed before.* Brethren, teach the whole Word of God to your people like you have never taught the Word before!"

That was all Brother Erickson could take. He began shouting, "Let's go pray! Let's go pray!" He turned and ran to his office with two of the other brothers trailing him. The other one just stood there, then asked, "Gerald, will you join us in prayer?"

I was surprised at his question. Didn't I always join them in prayer?

"Of course," I said smiling. "Let's go." I must act exactly as I would have one month before any of these strange happenings started, I reminded myself again.

By the time we entered the office, the other men were already on their knees. I knelt down and began to pray out loud. Leading out in prayer was something I had never done before without being asked, since I was the youngest and most timid of the bunch. After I finished, Brother Erickson started in with a long, loud, earnest prayer. One by one they prayed with an intensity I'd never heard before. When they all had prayed, Brother Erickson started in again. But before he could finish his prayer I interrupted.

"That is enough. Let us get up now."

Like obedient children, they immediately rose from their knees and sat on their chairs.

I opened my Bible to Acts chapter 2 and proceeded to read aloud the entire chapter. They listened intently.

After I finished, I rose to leave.

As I walked to the door the Baptist minister called after me, "Gerald, thank you so much for telling us about this."

I stopped in my tracks and faced them. "Brethren, this was not me speaking to you. This was my body you saw and my voice you heard, but this was from the Lord your God!"

I turned, shut the door behind me and got in my car. Seven miles down the road, at the exact same spot at which I'd felt the warm sensation come over me, I felt it leave in the same manner. Starting from my toes, it lifted slowly, finally vanishing through the top of my head and leaving a numb coolness in its place.

All of a sudden I became aware of all that happened. And I was embarrassed. Terribly embarrassed. What had those ministers thought of me? Thinking back, I remembered in detail all that I'd said and how I'd acted. That just wasn't like me. And the things I had said—I almost cringed.

But I hadn't said them. God had said them. And they were almost the same words Amos had used the night before.

"Dear Jesus, to think you saw fit to use me this way—" I marveled at what had just happened. Although I could totally recall all I had said and done, I also knew I had had absolutely no control over it. God had arrested my body for His use.

All at once I became dead tired. I felt as if I'd put in a long, hard day of physical labor and it became extremely difficult for me to even continue driving. All I wanted to do was sleep. The anointing had lifted.

Every one of those congregations represented at that

prayer meeting that morning, with the exception of the Nazarene, received an outpouring of revival.

For some reason during this time God saw fit to change all our names. He assigned names of Bible characters to each of the men who were in our home and we were to address each other by these names—Paul, John and Amos was Peter. I had not been assigned a name—until now.

It was later in the same day I had made my journey to Detroit Lakes. God spoke through one of the guests in my living room.

"Gerald, you are to choose your name," I was told simply.

A little taken aback that I was given the opportunity to choose my name, I answered, "Lord, you can give me whatever name you see fit."

"Would you accept 'Andrew'?" He answered.

"Yes. Yes, of course. 'Andrew' is fine," I replied.

So I became Andrew. He wasn't one of your more outstanding disciples, I noted, but upon some study of the Scriptures, I found that Andrew had a ministry of introduction, in that he introduced Peter to Jesus. In ensuing years, it became apparent that my own ministry would be one of introduction also. I would devote my life to introducing people to the wonderful blessings of Jesus Christ and the kingdom of God.

The awe-inspiring perfectness of God and His expectation of perfection from us was revealed constantly. Many times it was very strange and almost foolish, and usually it was frightening. On Thursday of that week, Mark Landes, one of the Mennonite ministers who had been involved in the initial stages of this revival in Loman, came to visit us. He had heard that God was doing some unusual things at our place and was eager to see for himself.

After greeting him warmly, we began to tell him all the strange and wonderful things that had been taking place. He listened closely with a look of amazement. In the midst of our conversation, the Lord suddenly spoke through someone in the room.

"You must pray," we were commanded. "Mrs. Dorsett is being severely tested and tried right now. Four of you are to kneel and pray earnestly, with weeping and wailing for seven minutes. Mark, you have a gold watch in your pocket you shall use to time these prayers."

Mamie Dorsett was a close and dear friend of ours. We quickly commenced to do as the Lord had told us. Four of us kneeled down and began to cry out to the Lord. Our wailing filled the room. Mark had taken off his watch and handed it to Johnny who was to keep time.

All at once Johnny exclaimed, "The watch has stopped! It's only been four minutes and the watch has stopped!"

Mark's head jerked up. "Why, I can't believe it. That watch always kept perfect time. It's been in the family for many years—in fact, it's a keepsake. It's always worked perfectly."

He took the watch from Johnny, looked at it, then held it to his ear.

"You're right. It's stopped," he said slowly.

Just then Amos spoke up. "The watch was stopped by Satan," he said. "It is unclean. Mark, what would you think if the watch would be destroyed?"

Mark looked at Amos. It was obvious that some other power was talking through Amos. "If it would be God's will for it to be destroyed, I would be willing. Perhaps I have had too much pride in that watch anyway—" his voice trailed off.

"Johnny," Amos said. "Take the watch into the basement. Then find the ax Gerald uses to split logs, and use it to smash the watch."

Johnny looked quickly at Mark. The heavy gold heirloom pocket watch dangled from his fingers. Mark laid the watch in Johnny's hand.

"Here. Take it and do as the Lord has told you," he said quietly.

Johnny closed his hand over the watch and walked down the stairs into the basement. We all waited upstairs, listening for the sound of the ax, and wondering what would come of all this.

The thudding sound of the blunt end of the heavy tool echoed up the stairs. Assuming the job had been completed, we waited for Johnny's footsteps.

Instead of that, we heard another thud. Then another, and another. The ax kept coming down. I couldn't believe that one blow with that heavy ax wouldn't totally demolish the delicate watch and everything in it.

For the fifth time we heard a thud. Then the sixth.

Then Amos spoke. "Freddy, go to the basement door and tell Johnny the next time he strikes the watch will be the last."

Fred hurried over to the top of the stairs and called down Amos's message.

The seventh blow of the ax was followed by the sound of tinkling parts flying in all directions.

Johnny walked up the steps into the living room, his face white as chalk. "It wouldn't break," he said, shaking his head. "It just wouldn't break. Every time I brought the ax down on it with all my might, it just bounced off. Then the sixth time I hit it, the watch stuck into the log sideways and the seventh blow shattered it."

Seven times. There it was again. God's perfect number. Far from being amusing or fun, it was fearfully sobering. Whenever anyone opened his mouth to relate a past experience or observation, God would speak through someone first and interject, "Are you absolutely certain you will be able to tell this *exactly* as it happened? If not, hold your peace."

We didn't open our mouths any more than we had to. Like children, we were disciplined whenever we reacted or behaved in any way that was less than obedient or perfect. We paid for every mistake. Our discipline took different forms. If someone was not absolutely punctual, he may have been ordered to scrub the floors. Or if someone had had a fleeting doubt about a particular experience he may have been instructed to skip a meal or do the dishes.

We were always being tested for our courage and total trust in what God was doing. He wanted no room whatsoever left for a fleck of unbelief. At times when Satan would be allowed to enter someone's body, they would hurl themselves at one of us, swinging their fists and acting in a hideously insane manner. But they would not be able to touch or harm us—if we did not flinch. Interestingly enough, Beulah was always able to hold her ground and look the possessed person squarely in the eye. But one time my gaze faltered and a fingernail gouged a nick in my chin. It was my fault. My faith had wavered and therefore I had suffered the consequences. A little scab eventually grew over the nick. Many times since, as I've gone through particularly difficult times, I have thought of that strange experience. It's a stinging reminder of my fallibility.

FOLLOWING THE FIRE

PHOTO SECTION

The Derstine family. Seated: Beverly Derstine, Jannette Derstine; Standing: Gerald Layman, Joanne Layman, Beulah Derstine, Rev. Gerald Derstine, Timothy Derstine, Philip Derstine; In tree: Stephen Derstine.

Mom and Dad Derstine,
Durell, Willie and Gerald.

Gerald as a high school sophomore.

Our wedding party.

Gerald, Beulah and Joanne in 1951 when Gerald was
pastor of Strawberry Lake Mennonite Church.

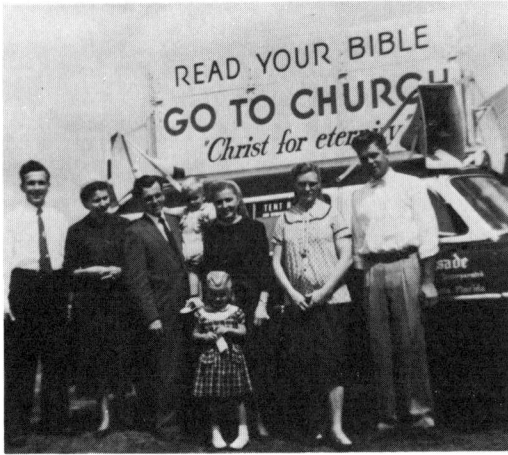

Tent meeting days. Left to right: Jack
and Rhoda Ann Fries; Beulah, Gerald and
the children; Amos and Joy Stoltzfus.

Our revival tent.

The tent fills with praise.

The storm's devastation.

Altar call under the tent.

Henry Brunk.

Grandpop Kauffman.

Christian Retreat, Bradenton, Florida.

The Tabernacle, Bradenton, Florida.

Inside the Tabernacle.

Minnesota Retreat Tabernacle.

Gerald and Beulah Derstine.

15

The Fire Melts Tradition

It was Friday night. I slipped a freshly starched, long-sleeved white shirt off a hanger and eased into it, then moved over to the bureau mirror and buttoned the shirt up to my neck.

"Are my gray socks clean, Beulah?" I asked, running a comb determinedly over the cowlick that refused to submit.

"Yes, they're right in your drawer," Beulah answered from where she was changing a diaper. "Gerry, do you really think we should go tonight?" She picked up the baby and walked over to the dresser. I talked to her reflection in the mirror.

"This is our usual prayer meeting night, you know, and I haven't been told not to go. In fact, just a few minutes ago I was instructed to go and moderate the meeting as long as I didn't say anything about what's happening here. Like when I went to Detroit Lakes the other day, God told me to act as I would one month before these things started happening—"

"But your voice. Why, you can hardly talk. How are you ever going to moderate a service?" Beulah worried.

"I know I really sound bad," I agreed. "But I have to go. If God wants me to talk He will just have to heal my hoarse throat; that's all." I put the comb down and walked over to the closet for my plain-cut coat. "Besides, God said there were going to be certain people there—" I hesitated telling her exactly who was to be in that service.

"What do you mean by 'certain people'?" she asked quickly, fixing her eyes on the back of my head. Now I had to tell her.

"Beulah, we were told that some ministers are going to be there. And along with those ministers, Rev. Hunsicher is coming."

"Bishop Hunsicher?" Beulah asked in dismay.

"Yes, he's the bishop all right. Evidently he's heard something's been going on and wants to come and see for himself."

"D-do you think he will understand, Gerald?" Beulah asked again.

Turning to look at her, I hesitated before answering her question. I wished she hadn't asked it.

"Why, I should think he would. He's been a leader in the church for many years and he knows the Bible much better than I do. And he will sense the same Spirit that has brought so many to the Lord in the past few months. Actually, I think he will be very happy to see what's going on."

Somehow, though, when I said that I had a disturbing feeling in the pit of my stomach. I dismissed it as butterflies at the prospect of having a superior in my congregation.

"I still don't see how you're going to moderate with that voice," Beulah said.

"You about ready to go?"

"Yes. I just have to get Joanne's coat and mittens on. The baby's all ready."

Fifteen minutes later I pulled the car into the church

parking lot. It was full—something that was very unusual for a Friday night. Leaving Beulah and the children to find their seats, I walked around to the front door and stepped out onto the platform. My eyes took a quick inventory of the sanctuary and came to rest on the row of ministers sitting next to Bishop Hunsicher. I wasn't surprised. So far God's words to us had been 100 percent accurate.

It was my usual practice to first greet the congregation, then lead in an opening hymn. I intended to follow this same procedure, all the while reminding myself to "do as you would have done one month before these things began to happen." But as I stepped up to the podium and opened my mouth, I felt a tremendous power surge through my body. It commandeered my mouth.

"The Lord our God is with us!" my voice rang out in crystal-clear tones. There was no sign of my hoarseness of a few moments ago. Vaguely aware of the visitors who sat stiffly near the back of the church, I continued to speak. In spite of my careful intentions to "act normal," I heard my voice telling everyone to turn to Acts, chapter 2. I proceeded to read passages about the great revival which is prophesied to come upon the earth. For ten minutes I preached with an anointing and fervor I had never experienced before.

"God is moving upon the earth in this day! He is pouring out His Holy Spirit upon all flesh. These are the last days and we must be ready!" On and on I went.

Suddenly, as I paused for an instant, another voice rang out over the congregation. "Let us get on our knees now and pray!" it announced. I stopped abruptly and noted that the voice belonged to one of my parishioners, a man who was normally quiet and timid. It was shocking for him to act in this assertive manner. But as a body, the people obeyed. The old wooden pews creaked and the muffled sound of knees settling themselves on the bare floor filled the room. I knelt in front of a pulpit chair and began to thank God for doing His works among us. Little by little the silently whispered prayers escalated into audible words, something uncharacteristic of our usual custom of praying silently to ourselves. Then the words became louder and the sounds turned into sobs and heart-wrenching wails. The volume was being steadily turned up as the intensity of our prayers increased. Finally after about ten minutes, we heard a voice raised above the din. It was the same man who had told us to get on our knees and pray.

"We must get up now and rejoice in the Lord!" his voice boomed as his arms raised upward. Just as suddenly as the praying had started, the noise ceased and only the sound of shuffling was heard as everyone stood up. Then they followed instructions. They began to praise the Lord. Hands came up, slowly and tentatively at first, then finally easing up till hands and faces strained toward the ceiling. Sounds of rejoicing filled the sanctuary and now that the bindings of tradition were loosened there was little problem in casting them to the wind. Like prisoners who after many years of confinement have finally been set free we reveled in our new-found liberty. We had become like children, filled with joy, freedom and hope.

Momentarily remembering the bishop and visiting officials, I opened my eyes and looked toward the back. The place where they had been sitting was vacant.

Before I had a chance to close my eyes again, the main

entrance door opened. Framed in the opening was Bishop Hunsicher. His eyes darted about the room for a few seconds, then he spoke in a loud voice. "You who are on the Lord's side, come out of there!"

A dense silence fell on the room. Hands came down slowly and people's heads looked to the floor. The bishop waited. But no one made a move. At that moment, I remember feeling sorry for him.

"Let us all sing and rejoice," were the next words we heard slicing evenly through the silence. The instructions came through the same one who had been giving them all evening. And they were instantly obeyed. To the jubilant strains of songs and shouts of praises, the bishop shut the door.

Now that they had committed themselves to following through with what God had told them to do, the people sang and rejoiced with even more fervor. Finally, one broke out into the aisle in a graceful dance. Then others followed on their toes. Their arms were upstretched, ed, and they were singing songs of praise to God. The women wore their white-net prayer coverings and the men were dressed in their plain, dark-colored suits. They glided lightly around the sanctuary, in between the pews, and up and down the middle aisle, completely oblivious to the pairs of eyes that peered cautiously into the side windows.

After this went on for a time, we were given another directive.

"Durell, you are to go outside and speak to the ministers. Tell them they may come in now and speak to the congregation."

My brother did as he was told, but the ministers refused to come in. In fact, they never did come back into the church that night.

Apologizing later, the bishop said they were indeed angered at the time by what they saw in the church and were sincerely convinced that we were being deceived by the devil. In fact, they were so convinced that they visited various members of our church in their homes and tried to talk them out of what they had experienced and encouraged them to go to another church.

As we lingered around the breakfast table the next morning, Amos, Johnny, Joy, Louise, Beulah and I discussed the events of the night before.

"Yeah, that was really somethin'," Amos was saying as he poured another glass of milk. "Those ministers disappeared out the back door so fast—" He shook his head and grinned to himself. "I wonder what they're thinking this morning."

"I'm sure they probably see everything in a different light now that they've had some time to think it over," I answered. "It must have been a shock to them to see us acting so emotionally."

"Want some more coffee, Johnny?" Beulah asked as she began to clear the table.

"No thanks," Johnny said. "Beulah, did you see the bishop walk out last night?"

"No, I guess I wasn't paying much attention," Beulah smiled. Her face grew solemn then. "I do hope they understand, though —"

Amos got up from the table and walked over to the sofa. He lay down, closed his eyes, and began to speak in tongues. After a few moments he gave the interpretation. It was for me.

"*Gerald, you are to be separated from the Mennonite*

church, but do not fear, for I shall give you a greater ministry. I will take you to the outer edges of the Mennonite communities. You shall minister to and teach many people about the things of my Spirit. Amos spoke calmly, slowly, but forcefully.

After the first sentence he had spoken, my mind began to race. *You shall be separated from the Mennonite church—* Why should that be? What had happened here this past week was what the church needed. Certainly they would be overjoyed to hear of this revival. I didn't want to separated from the church.

"But, Lord, what about the Mennonites?" I asked impulsively.

"Gerald, the Mennonites will not understand now but they shall later," I was told.

At that, my mind relaxed a bit. I could see how some of my friends and colleagues would not understand right at first. But surely in two or three weeks they would see that this was a work of God and would accept us. I supposed we could take that.

But Amos was not finished yet.

Gerald, I am going to take you into the cities. From city to city you shall go, ministering unto multitudes and thousands of my people, teaching them the things of my Spirit. Amos's voice stopped now and he lay there quietly, peacefully with his eyes closed like he was asleep.

I took a deep breath then went over to sit on the piano bench. It was hard to comprehend the words I had just heard. It was ludicrous to think that I, an unknown, little, simple Mennonite pastor, would be speaking to thousands of people. I didn't even know anyone in a big city. Besides, what would I have to say to anyone other than my own people? I wished Amos hadn't said those words. And I wished there hadn't been anyone else in the room.

Amos stirred now on the sofa. It creaked as he shifted his weight. There was a stack of bedding at one end of the sofa since all this week someone had to sleep on it for lack of bed space upstairs. Amos leaned over, grabbed one of the blankets and covered himself, up to his chin. It certainly wasn't cold in the room. The little furnace in the cellar roared fitfully and we usually had to close some of the vents so it wouldn't get too hot. I wondered why he felt the need for a blanket. It seemed strange.

Then without looking at me he said, "Play 'Up From the Grave He Arose.' "

Since I was the only piano player in the house I guessed he meant me. So I swung around and put my fingers on the keyboard. I knew the song by heart. Glancing across the room, I noticed Beulah standing in the archway between the living room and kitchen. She smiled faintly as she waited for me to start playing. I looked down at my hands and, starting with the verse, began to play the lovely melancholic melody. The others in the room began to sing, blending their voices in three part harmony. I held out the last arpeggio of the verse in preparation for the first strident, joyful notes of the chorus.

Then I played "Up from the grave He arose," savoring the exciting transition the song made from sad and somber to majestically exuberant. At that precise moment there was a flash of movement to my left. Amos leaped to his feet, throwing the blanket on the back of the sofa and with his arms and face lifted in the air, he began to dance around the room on tiptoes. His face glowed with the innocence and rapture of a child as his body floated effortlessly around the living room. The others were quick to join him. Beulah among them, and they sang the chorus again and again as they stepped lightly. Their eyes were closed but they never once stepped on the two children playing quietly on the floor. From the living room to the kitchen and back to the living room they glided while I played chorus after chorus. Little by little, my hands seemed to play the keys by themselves as I entered into the heavenly cloud of glory. The seven people dancing around the room didn't look like people any more. They were magnificent angels. And their voices were like the voices of angels, singing the song of the Lamb.

It was a celebration to end all celebrations. And unknown to us at the time, it was the grand finale of our supernatural, week-long visitation from God.

16

Silenced

That same Saturday evening God spoke through one of the boys, directing each one of us in the house. Beulah and I and the children, as well as Freddy, Johnny and Amos, were to go to the two-week Bible school that was scheduled in Loman, the same place where the youth Bible school had been earlier. The others in the house were instructed to go to various other places and by late that night the house was empty. We didn't know the revival had ended. We were just continuing to follow instructions. But as I paused in the kitchen before going out to the car and locking up the house, I felt strange. It was the first time in seven days the house had been empty. It was so quiet. The gaping holes yawning from the living room ceiling suddenly seemed out of place. I turned the key in the lock and we started out for Loman.

Since God's visitation to us had started at Loman we felt at ease about going back. I looked forward to being a participant in the Bible school rather than a teacher. There were so many things about the Bible that I wanted to dig into a little more. Besides that I wanted to tell my Mennonite friends there what had taken place at Strawberry Lake.

But when we arrived we discovered they had already heard what had happened at Strawberry Lake. And they weren't exactly thrilled. In fact, they didn't quite know how to handle us. Amos finally proved to be more than they could take. He was so radiant and visibly full of the glory of God that he frightened them. His public prayers were not properly quiet and controlled, but boisterous and powerful. Attempting to keep everything "decent and in order," the church officials finally urged Amos to leave. He did so, taking Freddy and Johnny with him. They traveled to Palmetto, Florida, where they had some friends.

Beulah and I took the two-week school, then returned home. After unlocking the door and walking through the kitchen, Beulah and I both stopped and stared in astonishment at the living room ceiling.

During the week's revival in our home my mother had lost sixteen pounds. She was so upset over what was happening to us she couldn't eat or sleep. She spent hours on her knees asking God to spare us from going entirely crazy. Although she hadn't been to the house all week, dad had come once and had seen the holes in the ceiling. When mom heard about that her worst fears had seemed to be confirmed.

Hearing we had left the house to go to Loman, she prevailed upon dad to fix the ceiling while we were gone. She would not step into the house until it was done.

So dad went to town, bought some new Celotex boards, removed what was left of the old squares, and put the new ones in place. When the job was completed, he went home to bring mom over to inspect the finished job.

Mom reluctantly agreed to come over. She walked in through the back door, went through the kitchen and stopped at the entrance to the living room. As she raised her eyes to the ceiling, the color drained from her face and she gasped. Down the full length of the ceiling was a perfect cross! The brand-new stark white tiles contrasted sharply with the older ones that had been grayed from long winter months of indoor heating. No one had noticed before that the holes in the ceiling had formed any particular pattern. Dad hadn't even noticed it when he fixed them. It was meant for mom. God was so mindful of her concern that He gave her a sign to give her the peace of mind she needed.

So it was that impressive white cross that we beheld as we stepped into our living room that day.

It wasn't long before we discovered that while we had been in Loman, Bishop Hunsicher had been circulating among my church members, questioning what they had experienced and suggesting I had been led astray by the devil. I was deeply hurt. The thought that someone I had so highly respected had betrayed me was overwhelming. If only he had come to me instead of my friends and parishioners. Yet I couldn't help but realize he was only doing what he felt had to be done. He wanted to spare my flock from what he thought was a misled fanatic. He was responsible as bishop over that district.

I was finally able to confront him with my feelings.

"Brother, I'm sorry, but I don't understand why you have gone to these people and said these things about me," I blurted out, suddenly feeling very young and awkward.

The older man's eyes at long last looked searchingly into mine. There was a long silence and I hoped he couldn't hear the thumping in my chest. I forced myself to hold his gaze. He took a deep breath.

"Gerald, I've heard about all that's happened and surely

you must realize we just can't accept it. You know the Mennonite church doesn't teach this sort of thing."

"I know it doesn't teach this sort of thing," I said. "But it happened! We were praying for revival and God gave us revival."

"But you must admit that a lot of strange things happened—devilish things according to some of the people I've talked to. I can't believe you could say they were from God," the bishop answered, leaning forward in his chair.

"Yes, I know a lot of strange things took place. And God did allow the devil to manifest himself periodically. But it was only as God allowed it. He had some purpose in it—some lesson to teach us, some point to bring across. God was always victorious and Satan was always defeated."

The bishop continued to ask questions but the sinking feeling in my stomach that he just was not going to understand steadily crept in. The blinders of hundreds of years of orderly tradition blocked the light from his eyes.

Finally he asked, "Gerald, if God wanted to bring some great revival to the Mennonite church or even as you say, to the world, why would He do it way out here in the sticks of northern Minnesota, in a little mission church nobody ever heard about? And why would He use you and that handful of teen-agers who are just barely Christians?"

It was an unfair question. And I had no answer. I had asked myself that same question a dozen times in the past couple weeks and, for all the pondering and analyzing, I hadn't been able to come up with an answer.

I shook my head and looked down at my shoes. "I don't

know; I just don't know."

Now all I wanted to do was get away from the questions. I had two more visits from my church authorities before my fate was decided. They were agonizingly painful visits, filled with searching questions and pregnant silences. The men were impressed with the courage I displayed at sticking with my story and they complimented me on my attitude. My past record with the church had been impeccable up to that point and they admitted this to me. But they just could not comprehend the phenomena that had just taken place and they had no alternative but to settle the situation in the only way they could see open to them.

It became apparent to me that it was useless to defend what had happened—there was so much of it I didn't understand myself. Yet I was firmly convinced that it had been sent by God—100 percent of it.

Trying to spare me, the church officials agreed to let me continue on as before if I would only admit that a percentage of this revival had been from the devil.

"Would you agree that perhaps 50 percent of what happened was not of God?" I was asked.

"No, I cannot agree with that," I answered.

"Would it be realistic to say 25 percent was caused by the devil?" was the next question.

"No, I'm sorry. I can't even say that," I replied.

"Surely you know that Satan was involved in some of the activities that went on. Can't you just admit that 10 percent was of the devil?"

I stood my ground. There was no question as to the truth in my mind. "No, I can't even say 10 percent was of the devil. God only allowed him to come in periodically, but it was all entirely directed of God." My voice was surprisingly calm and steady.

Their interrogation of me stopped at that and I knew my options were depleting fast. There was silence now, interrupted only by the ticking of a clock. The bishop leaned back in his chair and scratched the back of his neck before hunching forward again and looking directly into my eyes.

"Gerald, what shall we do with you?" the startling question was asked in utmost sincerity and an almost childlike bewilderment.

I now knew exactly what lay ahead. Into my mind flashed a picture of Amos lying on the sofa.

"Gerald, you shall be separated from the Mennonite church—"

I forced the picture from my mind and said, "Brethren, I am willing to give up my charge as pastor if you feel this will help you come to a decision." I couldn't believe I'd said it.

The meeting was dismissed at that, but several hours later the head bishop faced me with the verdict. His face was expressionless but the emotion he was trying to conceal escaped through the quiver of his voice.

"Gerald, we feel it is necessary that you be temporarily silenced from ministering in the Mennonite church both here and elsewhere. What you have permitted and practiced in your church and home is contrary to our church theology and doctrine and we must ask you to refrain from talking about it or teaching it. We will see how things develop and at a later time this action may change."

My mind had already gone back to the sofa in the living room. *But do not fear, for I shall give you a greater ministry. . . . from city to city you shall go and you shall minister to multitudes . . . . the things of my Spirit.*

Now that the decision had been made there were no more words to be said. I embraced my elder, wished him God's blessing and saw him to the door. Several days later I was given one more chance to redeem myself. I received a call from one of the church authorities.

"If you promise never to mention any of these things that you experienced from the pulpit, this restraint will be voided and you can continue on. You may believe in your heart, but you must not say anything publicly."

With a heavy heart, I declined the offer. We had come too far to turn back now. Besides, the prophecy had also said, ". . . the Mennonites will not understand now, but they shall *later*." I could wait several weeks. Or even months.

When I told Beulah what had happened, she wasn't surprised. The finality of it caused some apprehension since we had no idea of what our next step would be. But knowing it was of the Lord we soon began to rejoice in our situation, such as it was. Word spread of our dismissal and although many of our friends and church members were alarmed at what had happened, we assured them we were happy and that it would probably only be temporary anyway.

It wasn't long before we found out what our next step would be. It came in the form of a letter from Amos who was now in Florida. The letter looked very strange. Bold, red lettering stood out in vivid contrast to smaller blue handwriting. As I began to read, it became apparent that the dominant red scrawl was written in the same one-word-at-a-time style in which prophecy came to us during the week in our home.

It read, "Gerald, you must come to Florida. Your wife and two children should come along but no one else is to accompany you. . . . This letter is written in red to signify the blood of Jesus Christ. What I am writing is being directed by the power of the Holy Spirit and is the word of the Lord for you, Gerald. . . ."

Florida! I thought Florida was just a place where worldly people went to live a life of leisure. I'd certainly never considered going there. But as I folded up the letter, at the same time I felt a witness that this was indeed a word from the Lord. Beulah read the letter and felt the same way. We were both still close enough to the strange happenings of the revival that this didn't seem particularly unusual to us. This was the first directive we had received from God by way of mail, and this caused me a moment's hesitation, but I reasoned that Amos was in Florida—and we were in Minnesota, with no phones or other way of getting the message to us.

So we decided to go to Palmetto, Florida, where Amos had told us to go. By now all our guests had gone and although he hadn't given us a reason, we felt led to go and find out the reason when we got there.

The only problem was money. We had absolutely no money to make the long, 2,000-mile trip. I hadn't received a salary from the church in the first place so there was certainly no "severance pay" and the little money I earned from my Watkins route was barely enough to meet our living expenses. If God wanted us in Florida, He would have to perform a miracle in some way to give us the money.

At that point I wouldn't have been the least surprised to find the money growing on a tree in our back yard or to find it in the mouth of a fish I caught out of the lake. I'd read in the Bible somewhere that Peter had found coins in a fish's mouth.

However, after praying about it, I felt impressed to go to the bank and ask to borrow $100, the minimum amount I figured it would take. The only thing that worried me was what I was going to tell the banker when he asked why I was going to Florida.

I decided to give it a few more days. Maybe the money would come in the mail.

But the money didn't come that way and I began to seriously consider going to the bank. I anticipated what the conversation would be like:

Banker: "Well, Mr. Derstine, why do you need to borrow $100?"

Me: "We're planning a trip to Florida."

Banker: "Oh? Why are you going to Florida? Vacation?"

Me: "No, we're going because the Holy Spirit told us to go."

Banker (with funny look on his face): "Holy Spirit? I see. For how long did He tell you to be there?"

Me: "He didn't tell us yet. We'll have to find out when we get there."

Banker: "You do know Florida is a big place. Where exactly are you going there? Will you have a job?"

Me: "We don't know that yet either."

I wasn't looking forward to this. Well, Lord, if this is what you want me to do, you'll have to handle it. I'll just have to tell him the truth. I figured if worse came to worse I could pay the $100 back to the bank by washing dishes in a diner along the way, or by pumping gas, or something else of that sort.

Gathering up my courage, I tried to make myself look confident as I kept my appointment to see the loan officer.

He smiled politely when I walked in and I was relieved

to see that he seemed friendly. I took the chair he offered after we shook hands and got right to the point.

"Sir, I would like to borrow $100." Best to start out by saying as little as possible. Keep it short and concise. Don't offer any information that's not asked.

"One hundred dollars? Fine. How would you like to repay the loan—by the month or in one lump sum?"

My mouth dropped open before I could mask the surprise that registered on my face. Quickly regaining my composure, I answered, "I'll pay it back in one lump sum. Would you give me six months?" I figured within six months surely I would be able to earn enough somewhere to pay back the $100.

"That's fine. Just sign here," he said, shoving the necessary papers across the desk.

That was it. No more questions. I walked out of the bank with the $100, shaking my head in disbelief. I had done business before with that bank and this was definitely not their normal procedure. Never had I, nor anyone I knew, taken out a loan with so little effort. Well, Lord, I should have known you'd come through—

Now, like the Israelites of old, we would follow the fire through the night. Frightened, yet confident that as long as we kept our eyes on the pillar of fire we would be safe.

I stuffed the wad of bills into my pocket and jumped in the car to go home and tell Beulah.

17

Called to Florida

"Want to check the house one more time before we go just to make sure we got everything?" I asked Beulah from our packed-to-the-ceiling car with the motor idling.

"Yes, I guess I should," Beulah agreed, helping Joanne into the back seat and adjusting Philip on the front. She hurried back into the house, took one last check, then came out and closed the door behind her, turning the key in the lock. I noticed she was carrying a big brown paper sack.

"Almost forgot the sandwiches and fruit I packed for us to eat on the way," she said, breathlessly climbing into the seat beside me.

It's a good thing I always ask her to check one more time, I thought. Seems like she remembers everything— until we're five miles down the road.

I smiled over at her as I remarked, "Oh, you made some sandwiches? Great! I think I'm hungry."

"Dad! We just ate," she laughed.

Moments later we were on our way to Florida. Convinced God had told us to make the journey, we put our fears and anxieties behind us and now all that remained was an exciting anticipation.

It had been hard at first. Even after we had gotten the money to go, we had our family and some of our well-meaning friends to contend with. Of course mom and dad were worried, but by now they knew we would obey what we felt God had told us—whatever it was.

Durell, my brother, had said, "Gerald, how can you jeopardize your whole family? You could have a car wreck and be killed. I can see maybe your going if you felt you had to, but why take your whole family?" He was genuinely worried.

"Durell, I'm afraid *not* to go. If I don't obey God I'm afraid my house may burn down—with all of us in it!"

We had no idea what awaited us in Florida. I figured if we ran out of money I could always get some odd jobs so we'd have enough food to eat and enough gas for the car. We could even sleep in the car if we had to.

As we made our way south, the snowy, icy roads gave way to firm, dry macadam. We rejoiced and sang the whole way, not even stopping to rest. We simply weren't tired.

There were only a few people we knew in Florida. The one I thought of first was a Mennonite minister and tent evangelist. He was an on-fire Mennonite in those days and his meetings produced many true salvation experiences. I had looked up to this man for years for his dynamic, effective ministry and now I wanted him to be the first to know about our outpouring of the Holy Spirit. I just knew he'd be thrilled and could hardly wait to share with him.

There was one other couple I knew. This Mennonite couple, the Detweilers, lived in northern Florida so we decided to make their home our first destination.

After welcoming us, the Detweilers pressed us for details on the revival. We talked at great length and they listened in awe. Afterwards, they asked us to join them at a special meeting their local Mennonite church was having. The minister, they said, was especially interesting and inspiring. His name was Linford Martin; he was from Sarasota, Florida.

When we were introduced to Brother Martin, we were surprised to learn he had already heard of some of the things that had taken place in our church. And to our delight, he wanted to know all about it. He listened with great interest to our story.

"Brother Gerald, this is just amazing. I can see without a doubt that God has visited you and poured out His Spirit on you. But where are you going from here?" he asked.

"Oh, we're on our way to Palmetto," I answered. "Brother Brunner has a work down there and I just can't wait to tell him what's happened!" Linford got a funny look on his face. A frown creased his brow and I stopped short.

"What's the matter?"

"Gerald, I don't think you'd better talk to Brother Brunner," he said slowly.

"Why not?" I stammered. "He will be so glad to hear how God is moving! The way he preaches I just know he's going to want to rejoice along with us."

"No, really, I don't think you should tell him these things yet," Linford countered. The tone of his voice disturbed me. I couldn't understand why he was so sure of himself.

"Look, Gerald, why don't you come on down to Sarasota where I live? It's close to Palmetto anyway. I have an empty house trailer where you and your family can stay, and I'll even give you a job working with me in construction if you like. How about it?"

"Really?" I was overjoyed. "Sounds like an answer to prayer. I don't know much about construction, but I do need a job. I'll talk to Beulah and we'll come on down."

"Great! It's settled then. Can you come tomorrow?"

"Sure, brother. See you then!" I stuck out my hand and he took it in a firm grip.

I went to find Beulah to tell her what had happened. She was relieved to know at least we'd have a place to stay.

"There was something strange, though," I told her. "When I told Brother Martin we were going to see Brother Brunner, he got this funny look on his face and told me we shouldn't tell him about what's happened in Minnesota. I can't understand why—"

"Well, maybe he's heard some things that aren't true," Beulah answered. "You know how rumors fly."

"If that's the case, all the more reason we should talk to him. When he hears the facts he will be overjoyed. I just know it!"

"But if Brother Martin said you shouldn't talk to him, maybe you should wait," Beulah remarked.

"No, I want to talk to him right away. We'll just stop by on our way to Sarasota." My mind was made up. "He may even have some direction from the Lord for us."

The next day we drove on down to Palmetto but found no one home. So we found the trailer house we were to live in and began to unpack our things. Although the living area of our new little home that sat under a canopy of mossy pines and oaks was considerably diminished, we were glad to know we were right where God wanted us. Beulah wasted no time in fixing up beds for the children and scrupulously cleaning out the cupboards and corners.

A few days later I set out for Palmetto so see Brother

Brunner. He was home this time, and welcomed me warmly as he invited me into his house. My heart was pounding rapidly and I eagerly launched into an account of what had taken place in Minnesota.

I had barely gotten started when to my surprise my friend leaped out of his seat and glared down at me, his features contorted with anger.

He shook his finger in my face and shouted, "Shut up! You can stop talking that nonsense right now or get out of here. I mean it—I don't want to hear any more of that junk!"

I couldn't have been more stunned than if a baseball bat had just slugged me. My mouth hung open and I stared into his darkened eyes. He really meant it!

"Junk? Why this isn't junk. It happened and God made it happen! Don't you understand? God spoke to us. There were people saved—"

"I believe in holiness!" the man interrupted. "I don't want to hear any more of what you're talking about. You can just leave if you're going to talk any more about it!"

I got up slowly and wordlessly walked from the room and out to my car. A profound feeling of despair and rejection engulfed my being. I suddenly felt dizzy. This just couldn't be. How could such a great man of God not want to even hear of something so incredibly powerful and glorious? He, of all people, should understand. And I had been so sure he would understand and rejoice along with us—perhaps answer some questions of my own.

I stumbled into the car and put my head down on the steering wheel. God, what should I do now? I thought you wanted me to talk to him and now there is no one, no one I can talk to and share with. I drove home slowly, dreading to tell Beulah what happened. Yet, for some reason, I had the feeling she wouldn't be too surprised.

The next day I began working for $1.40 an hour as a hod carrier, mixing mortar for cement blocks. It was hard work but good pay and I was grateful. And the first opportunity I had, I cornered Linford and told him what had happened with Brother Brunner. He nodded his head and took a deep breath.

"I know, Gerald. I tried to warn you, but I guess it was just as well you saw for yourself. You see after what he's gone through with Amos—"

"What do you mean? What does Amos have to do with this?" I interrupted.

He looked up at me in surprise. "Oh, you didn't know?" He pursed his lips and shook his head slowly. "Amos is in the hospital—fifth floor, psychiatric ward."

When he saw my mouth drop open he was quick to add, "It's a long story—and I can't really blame Brother Brunner for being frightened."

"I want to hear it," I said, thinking of the letter in bold red ink that had brought Beulah and me down here in the first place. "What's Amos doing in the hospital?" Of all people, I couldn't picture big, strong, gregarious Amos lying in a sterile hospital bed. "Is he sick or was he in an accident? No, you said psychiatric ward. Why in the world would he be there?"

"I guess you could say he had an accident of sorts. He got stabbed—"

"Stabbed? You mean cut with a knife?" I gasped.

"Yes, but he'll be all right, I think. He did get cut up pretty badly. But let me start from the beginning," Linford said as he pulled his chair closer to mine.

"You see, when Amos came down here and told Brother Brunner all that had happened in Minnesota, he wasn't quite prepared for the reception he got—I mean the same reaction you got. You know yourself that Amos is acting quite a bit different these days and I guess Amos just rubbed the man the wrong way. At any rate Amos was terrifically burdened for him because of this and spent days fasting and praying about it. He would call Brother Brunner at two or three in the morning and give him words from the Lord. I guess it didn't go over too well. But that's how Amos has been acting since he's been here— he's different. Kind of like he's being directed personally by God—that's what he says anyway. Sounds very convincing.

"Anyway, the other night he was out walking along a road in Ellenton when he felt suddenly impressed to go up to a certain house, knock on the door and cast some demons out of a man who lived there. You know how he claims he can see the powers of God and Satan in people. Now he didn't know who lived in that house but that didn't stop him. You have to admire his unquestioning obedience to what he feels God is telling him to do, that's for sure.

"So Amos went up to the house and walked into the screened porch. It was dark and he couldn't see too well in there and he accidentally bumped a glass jar that was on a shelf. Before he could knock, the jar crashed to the floor and a moment later the door flew open. There was a big black man standing there and before he could say anything Amos reached out his hand to place it on the man's head like he normally would do to cast a demon out of someone.

"Well, I guess the man thought Amos was going to hit him or something because from out of nowhere he produced a knife and started slashing away at Amos. He worked him over front and back—had him on the floor and he would have killed him if the man's wife didn't yell at him to stop.

"Amos was a mess by the time someone got him to the hospital. Nearly dead, they said. He lost a tremendous amount of blood and was thrashing around so much they had to straitjacket him. They got him all bandaged up, but when they wanted to give him blood transfusions he wouldn't let them. He said, 'Just give me seven glasses of water.' Can you believe it? He absolutely refused to let them give him any blood, and he was so persistent about the water that they finally gave it to him. Seven glasses. He drank it, and do you know he never did need a blood transfusion?

"Anyway, he kept asking for Brother Brunner. Over and over again he kept calling for him. We got the word to him and he finally came—reluctantly, that is. Amos was thrilled to see him and he immediately told Brother Brunner to strike him three times on the forehead. Now isn't that strange? He was very adamant about it and insisted that Brother Brunner follow his instruction. He said God had told him that if Brother Brunner would do that he'd be instantly healed. Well, no matter how much he insisted, Brother Brunner refused to do it. He walked out of that hospital room and started home. But that wasn't the end of it. On his way home he stopped at a store to pick up a few things and do you know he passed out cold right there in the store. I don't know, it sure seems funny to me, the whole story—"

"Is Amos still in the hospital?" I asked finally.

"Yes, he's still there. I guess they put him in the mental ward because they couldn't figure him out. I really feel sorry for him. He's recovering from the knife wounds all right."

"I'll have to go and see him right away," I said, standing up.

"I don't know if they'll let you in. They keep that place locked up pretty tight on that floor."

"They'll let me in. I'm a minister and I'm Amos's close friend. They'll have to let me in," I answered. "Oh, and by the way, that thing about him wanting Brother Brunner to hit him three times on the head has an explanation. During the revival, that was the standard procedure for us to use on Amos when he needed deliverance from a particularly rough battle with Satan. One of us was told to strike him on the forehead three times—one for the Father, one for the Son, and one for the Holy Ghost. Don't ask me why. That's just the way it was. And it always worked. So I really do believe that if Brother Brunner had done that to Amos in the hospital room he wouldn't be there today. He'd be home and perfectly well."

"Ah-h-h, that explains it then," Linford answered slowly.

The first chance I got I made a beeline for the hospital. After explaining I was a minister and close friend, they let me in to see Amos. But a nurse stopped me at the door. She looked at me like she wanted to say something but didn't quite know how to say it.

"Yes?" I said, looking at her.

"Reverend, this man is supposed to be crazy," she said, "but I don't think he is. I've been around him quite a bit and the only thing that I see that may be a little odd is that he talks about God a lot, but he seems rational and even friendly. I'd like it if you'd evaluate the situation and give me your opinion."

"Surely," I answered. I pushed open Amos's door and walked in.

"Gerry! Praise the Lord!" Amos shouted the instant he saw me.

I breathed a sigh of relief. "Amos! How are you?" His face was paler than usual and his chest was all bandaged up. But it was the same Amos.

"Aw-w, they got me stuck in this hospital and they're always tryin' to give me these pills and stick me with needles. I been goin' along with them so's to make it easier. But they won't give me a Bible. Now that bothers me. Say, Gerald, it sure is good to see you!" He sobered abruptly and stared at my face intently. A wide grin spread across his face. "I see you still have that nick on your chin," he said.

My hand automatically came up to my chin and felt the scab that had formed there. Had it been that short a time since the circumstances accompanying that reminder of my human imperfectness had happened? It seemed ages ago. And the vessel God had used to test my faith was the same person who was lying in bed swathed in gauze and smelling sterile. It seemed unreal.

We talked about what had happened in Minnesota and Brother Brunner and about our trip down to Florida. Amos told me the whole story of how he'd ended up in the hospital saying, "Gerald, I was only doing what the Lord told me to do. I sure didn't expect it to end up like this—but I'm feeling much better now and I really want to get out. I called my dad up in Pennsylvania and he's coming down to pick me up and take me home for a while. I don't really want to go but I guess I should—"

Before I left, I took Amos's hand and prayed for him. The nurse met me at the door. "Well? What do you think?"

"He's perfectly normal," I said. "Nothing at all wrong with his mind."

Two days later his dad came to pick him up and drive him home. The hospital released him on the condition that he continue to take his medication. However, the pills seemed to have an adverse effect on Amos and every time he took them he'd have a violent reaction. When I visited him he told me the pills made him feel strange and he hated having to take them.

In the car on the way to Pennsylvania his father insisted he stay on the medication and the violent phases continued until finally one day Amos managed to grab the pills and throw them out the window. This just reinforced his family's fears that he indeed was crazy and when they got him home they compelled him to stay in the basement, locked in.

However, Amos was eventually able to break out of a small window that was at ground level. He had a sudden urge to go to Minnesota. And he had to go as fast as possible. But he had no money. Remembering an uncle who lived close by, he set out to see him. Perhaps he would be able to lend him enough money to get to Minnesota. Sure enough, his uncle had just happened to receive $300 in payment for some eggs he'd sold and he handed it over to Amos. After Amos left he couldn't figure out why he felt so good about giving him the money.

Amos arrived in Detroit Lakes and began to hitchhike the last twenty-five miles to Strawberry Lake where Joy lived. They had been corresponding since he'd been in Florida. He hadn't been thumbing long when a deputy stopped his car and offered him a ride to where he was going. Unbeknownst to either of them at the time it was the same man who had been sent out to check up on us during those supernatural seven days and nights.

When Amos knocked on the Dodds' door several minutes before nine, he was greeted first by eyes wide with surprise, then joyful hugs—especially from Joy. She threw her arms around his neck, her long flaming red hair spilling over her shoulders.

"I knew you'd make it! I just knew you'd be here!" she exclaimed over and over.

"What do you mean?" Amos asked. "I didn't tell you I was coming. How did you know I'd be here? How could you know anyway?"

"Amos, I told the Lord you just had to be here by nine tonight or I was going to forget about everything. The revival, the funny things that happened, you, everything. I was just having so many doubts about the whole thing. Gerald and Beulah are gone, Freddy, Johnny, you—everyone was gone and people around here are saying it was of the devil and we're all crazy. Amos, you just can't imagine how it's been. Finally, I just told the Lord I had to see you and it had to be soon. I told Him if you weren't here by nine o'clock tonight—oh, Amos, I just can't believe it!"

There it was again. God's perfect timing coming through in flying colors. But why not? It was the same God who had synchronized the entire universe. He's the Master of perfect timing.

Soon after, Amos and Joy were married in a small Baptist church there in the north woods of Minnesota.

It was during this time while I was in Florida that I met someone who would have a tremendous effect on the rest of my life. Linford first told me about him.

"Gerry, there's someone I want you to meet. His name is Henry Brunk. He's in Haiti right now but when he gets back I want you to talk to him."

From his name, I knew he was probably a Mennonite. A little uncertain about them at this point I asked, "Is he from our people?"

"Yes, he is. But I'm almost sure you're going to get a much better reception from him than from some of these others you've talked to. He's a businessman, a building contractor. A quite successful one, I might add. He built the Tuttle Mennonite Church here in Sarasota and has built many housing developments. Henry's not a young man, but he has a burden for missions, particularly in the country of Haiti, and has started a work there. In the past several years God has really done something in his life and he has an intense desire to move ahead in the things of God. You'll like him, and I'm sure he's going to want to hear about the Minnesota revival."

I was interested. "Sounds tremendous." I ached for fellowship with brothers of my own faith who would understand. My encounter with Brother Brunner was still fresh and the wound was still smarting.

My meeting with Henry Brunk a few days later was all Linford had said it would be and more. After I finished my story of what had happened to me in recent weeks, Henry sat there weeping.

Through his tears he explained, "Gerald, this is an answer to prayer. You have been sent from God as an answer to my prayers. I know God has sent you—" Henry went on to say how he'd been recently born-again after forty years of being a church member. He and his wife and a few other couples took a five-month leave of absence from their jobs just to pray and seek the Lord. During this time God told Henry to go to Haiti, a place he never even knew existed before. After years of making money for himself, he now wanted to share it with others. Hence, his mission work in Haiti.

From that day on our hearts were knit closely together. Henry and his wife, Nora, took our family under their wing and made it possible for us to get started in full-time ministry. Now we knew the reason God had sent us to Florida. Henry and I have been working together from that day until this. He's in his eighties and still going strong.

18

On Becoming a Worm

"Beulah, before we really decide to go out into the evangelistic ministry, I feel we must go back to Minnesota." I got up from my pajama-clad knees where I'd just finished my usual bedtime prayers and eased myself under the covers. The trailer's tiny bedroom was illuminated only by the small, plastic-shaded lamp on the night stand. The children, tucked into their bunk beds in the next room, had ceased their sleepy chatter and drifted to sleep. Beulah's eyes were closed but I knew she wasn't sleeping. They opened now and she turned her head to me in the soft light.

She knew what I was going to say but I went on anyway.

"I have to find out if things are really finished for me there. Maybe by now everything will be all right—" I stopped searching for the right words, then went on. "Those people up there, they're not only friends and members of the church, but they're almost like, well, like family. I can't let them down."

"I know, "Beulah answered quietly. "I know exactly what you mean. God did send us there in the first place and then after all that happened in the church surely there must be a purpose for it all."

"Then you feel we should go back too?" I asked.

"Yes, I think we would both feel better about things," she replied as she clasped her hands behind her head on the pillow.

I breathed a sigh of relief and Beulah reached over and switched off the light. The crickets outside the trailer were in full voice and they sounded like an electrical hum in a defective P.A. system.

Beulah had the same attachment I had to the Mennonites and I was glad to discover I wasn't alone in my reluctance to admit our separation from them had been final. Besides, God had told us they would understand "later" and it had been several months. They'd had time to think it over and maybe were just waiting for us to return so we could answer some of their questions. I wondered what Garbers, and Louise, and Joy were doing. And I wondered who was bringing the little Fenley children to Sunday school. And I wondered who was standing behind the plain wooden pulpit on Sunday mornings.

The next morning we made our plans. Beulah's mother in Pennsylvania was getting married after many years of widowhood so we decided to go to Minnesota by way of Pennsylvania. While we were in that state I saw a friend of mine, the minister who led me into the sanctification experience in my early Christian life. Delighted to see me, he asked me to give my testimony in his Brethren in Christ church. After a moment's hesitation I agreed, having no way of knowing what lay in store for me that night. It was something I will never forget.

It was a Wednesday evening and the church was full. Besides the regular church members, some Mennonites had come in, curious to hear the Minnesota story. This was the first time I would be giving a public account of our strange experiences. Although I was a little apprehensive about speaking in front of strangers, I found myself eager to share with people who could accept what had happened as from God and be excited along with us about it.

As I stepped up to the lectern which was on the main floor in front of the congregation I glanced around. Beulah, with her usual smile of encouragement, was there, but I thankfully recognized no one else other than the pastor. This wasn't going to be as frightening as I'd thought. I took a deep breath and began to speak.

I started from the beginning with the visitation to the young people at the Bible school in Loman. Then I went on to describe what had happened in the Strawberry Lake church and finally in my home. The words came easily as I became engrossed once again in the same Spirit that had enveloped us those seven days and nights. The deeper I got into the events of that week, the more acutely unworthy I found myself becoming. I verbally interjected that observation into my testimony. It finally progressed to the point where this sense of absolute unworthiness overwhelmed me. Why God had chosen simple, insignificant people like us to pour out His Spirit upon in such a tremendous way was looming as a preposterous incredibility at that moment.

The next thing I became aware of was that my knees were giving way and my whole body was becoming limp. Feeling like I was in a dream, I felt as if I was floating to the bare floor. Nobody said a word and no one made a move to help me. Then I felt my body begin to slowly squirm. Inching along the floor I writhed until my fingers touched the edge of a rug runner attached to the floor. I found myself determined to squeeze myself under that rug and my fingers tried to dig under the runner. Not realizing it was tacked down, I persisted in trying to pry it up from the floor so I could get my head and body underneath it.

As I was doing this, I slowly saw some huge letters materialize in front of my eyes. The letters made a word, but they were so monstrous that I saw only one letter at a time until the whole word blazed like a colossal billboard. First I saw a "W." Following that an "O" appeared. Then an "R" emerged and finally the letter "M." WORM. That was all. And that was what I was at that moment—a worm.

In the distance I heard a lone man's voice say softly, "Praise the Lord." Strangely enough, I was still conscious of my surroundings. I knew I was in church, and I knew I was supposed to be speaking. There were people sitting out there. But at the moment I was unembarrassed by my actions.

After I gave up hopes of getting under the rug, I concentrated on getting myself back up on my feet. I grabbed onto the front bench, pulled myself up to my knees, then draped my arms over the back of the pew. As I rested there momentarily, a Bible verse came to me: "But we are all as an unclean thing, and all our righteousnesses are as filthy rags" (Isa. 64:6).

Somehow I got back on my feet and finished my message. It wasn't until I sat down next to Beulah that I became aware that I had acted strangely. In a flash it all came back and then I was deeply humiliated. I glanced at Beulah out of the corner of my eye but she looked straight ahead. These people probably thought I was losing my mind. I didn't blame them. I must have looked a sight, squirming around on the floor like that, but I couldn't help it. It happened, just like the things in Minnesota happened. I just hoped Beulah understood. I'd explain it to her when we got home.

As I sat there reminiscing over what had happened, my embarrassment slowly gave way to enlightenment. God began to minister to me in a sweet and gentle way. He had allowed this to happen to illustrate to me that no matter how crude and humble the vessel, He was big and mighty enough to use that vessel if He saw fit. An omnipotent God in a pot of clay, or a worm, or a heap of rags. The ultimate definition of humility—He let me experience it.

A hand touched my arm and rested there. Beulah's eyes still stared straight ahead, but her touch told me all I needed to know. I wouldn't have to explain.

It was three months before our family returned to "normal" after the revival hit us, and we felt ourselves gradually revert to the natural life style we had known prior to the visitation.

In most places it was already summer, but our Minnesota woods were only beginning to burst into spring. And it always made summer worth waiting for. Dazzling sapphire skies, zillions of delicate newborn leaves greening the trees and drinking-water pure lakes that still felt like ice even though they were no longer solid. The wood ticks and friendly mosquitos that were nearly big enough to carry you away did not matter. They were a small price to pay for the glorious celebration of spring's cautious but warm arrival.

As we pulled off the dirt road into the lane, our little home nestled in a clump of trees was a wonderfully welcome sight. Joanne, who was standing on the hump between the front and back seats, began bouncing up and down.

"Where 'Porty?" she squealed into my ear, leaning forward and looking for her friend, the big black Labrador.

"He's with Grandma, honey," Beulah replied. "We'll see him soon. Gerry, look at that garden. If we're staying here I know where I'm going to be spending some time."

"It does look pretty sad, doesn't it," I agreed. "M-m-m, but just look at that rich, black soil. Won't take long to get some nice vegetables from that."

"And raspberries, and rhubarb and maybe some sunflowers over there in the corner too," Beulah finished.

I opened my mouth to say, "Just don't go planning too much before we find out about the situation since we left," but thought better of it and decided to face the problem when it presented itself. Besides, I was already having visions of getting the ax out of the basement and clearing out a few dead trees out back and planting some peonies next to the front porch. Might even get my pole out and check out my tried-and-true fishing spots on Strawberry.

Settling back into our little home, it was hard to imagine the events of a few months earlier. There were no visitors there waiting for us, the holes in the ceiling were gone and the children romped noisily through the house. Only the cross running the length of the ceiling remained as a poignant reminder.

But the visit we received from the bishop several days later was a jolting confirmation that things would never again be the same. Even though we were given one last chance.

"Gerald, we are going to have a communion service at

the church tonight. Many of those who had been involved in the goings on at your home are going to make a public confession that what happened was of the devil. They will then be recognized once again as functioning members of the church." He looked up at me.

"You may join them if you wish to remain as pastor of this church."

I couldn't say anything. For an instant I knew how Jesus felt when His closest brethren deserted Him in the Garden. He was utterly alone. And now I knew my time had come to be alone. It's too hard, Lord! I can't bear it. How can my dearest and closest brothers and sisters desert me like this? Why must I be so absolutely sure this whole thing is of you?

But do not fear, for I shall give you a greater ministry. Ah yes, I remembered those words once again. Were they meant for a time like this? The words seemed vague and incomprehensible, yet comforting in a way.

There were no alternatives now. The die was cast. Gerald Derstine was a "peewee" again—in the eyes of the church, his friends, and his family.

But the master gardener was only pruning this scraggly tree down to size so it could begin to flourish. He had set the stage for a brand-new production. Could I have foreseen then just how radically my life would change from that point, I'm sure I would have been chastised severely for my unbelief.

What I remember most about the bleak, chilly Sunday night a few weeks later was the darkness. Sitting in my favorite easy chair by the frosty living room window, I looked out into the blackness. I wanted to lose myself in that cocoon of anonymous stillness. And yet, for all the absence of sound, my head was reeling with a tumult of emotions.

Just for a moment I allowed myself to revert to the scene that was unfolding a quarter mile down the road at the little church I so dearly loved. I could see Jim stand slowly then sit down. Ruth was next. Then William and Edith. One by one they were denying God's strange and powerful visitation to them in my home a few weeks earlier. O God, how could they do it? These people I loved, most of whom I had led to the Lord myself and who had gone through all this with me; they were assenting it had been a work of the devil. All for the privilege of remaining members of the church. Had I made better Mennonites than Christians?

The words of my superior played like a tape recorder through my thoughts. "Gerald, I know you believe what you have gone through was of God, but it's just not the Mennonite way—you know that. We don't believe in those things you say happened to you. We can't accept it.

". . . We're going to have to silence you from the Mennonite church and ask you not to minister any longer. . . "

I remembered when the bishop first talked to me and how I felt then. Firm in my convictions and deep-down peace, I knew I was doing the right thing. In fact, I was even able to smile when it was all over. The words he had spoken were bombshells, but the Lord mercifully seemed to transform them into marshmallows.

In years to come I would learn what Paul meant in 1 Corinthians 2 when he compared carnal Christians to spiritual Christians. It is so difficult for the carnal or natural man to accept anything new. It is foolishness to him. Our people rejected our experience because it had never happened before and therefore they reasoned it must have been of the devil.

But God is Creator and He does things new. It takes spiritual Christians to understand the things of the Spirit. Those of us who had been seriously praying and fasting for revival before it happened were the ones who remained faithful.

Now on this darkest of nights little imps of self-pity and uncertainty tugged at my insides. Was I *really* sure? Here I was cast into a totally unfamiliar world, while my closest friends, family members and parishioners turned their backs and crawled back into their secure little nests. I wished Amos were here. He would stand by me. But he was back in Pennsylvania.

Beulah was probably weeping in the next room. She felt the same agony I was enduring. She not only felt it for herself, but she felt it for me. I wanted to cry too. Big sobs that said, "Why me, God?"

But men aren't supposed to cry.

It was then that I heard the singing. A multitude of joy-filled voices, singing "Leaning on the Everlasting Arms," belonged to ministering angels who sang away the doubts and sadness and fear. A peace that passes all understanding settled over my spirit.

"Beulah, I'll be out for a while," I called into the kitchen the next afternoon.

"Where to? Well, don't go far. Supper will be ready around five." Beulah answered from over potato peelings flying from her fingers into the sink.

"I'll be back. I'm just going for a little walk."

It was a nice day for a walk. Not that I made a practice of taking walks. My exercise usually consisted of accomplishing something more than just enjoying the sunshine. That was why it was only an excuse. I wanted to take one last look at Strawberry Lake Mennonite Church before we set out for Florida the next day.

There was still a nip in the air but the sun shone clearly. The tops of the trees swished softly in the gentle afternoon breeze. I walked along the side of the road so I could observe which of the wildflowers and foliage had begun to emerge. The tall, stiff weeds in the ditch camouflaged, but could not hide, the delicate Queen Anne's lace and furry, dove-gray pussy willows. Dandelions huddled together in droves like golden blobs of creamery butter. The dandelions had already taken over our yard and I ruefully conceded the grass needed cutting. Beulah had just reminded me of that fact this morning. On down the road, a couple of dogs cavorted, the lower part of their bodies blending into the tall grass.

Suddenly at the top of the hill the dense woods gave way to a clearing and I was there. The plain, square-built church building which had always welcomed me with its familiar face still looked familiar and friendly. I wished it didn't. As I walked toward the front door I concentrated on disentangling myself from the comfortable bonds that had knit me to this place. It wasn't easy. But it had to be done. I wasn't welcome here any more. All I had to do now was say, "Good-bye."

My feet mounted the front steps that led to the door and I stopped. It was impossible not to notice the ugly crack that had split the door as the Carltons exited in such a fury several months ago. The crack, like the cross, was an eerie reminder of the strange thing that had brought me to this point.

I grasped the doorknob, turned it slowly and let myself

into the sanctuary. The setting sun streamed boldly through the uncovered windows and lit up the austere oak pews as if to contribute a bit of adornment to their plain, scrubbed, functional design. My footsteps made a hollow echo on the bare floor as I walked to the front where the pulpit stood. Cautiously, I stepped up and positioned myself behind the desk. It was a nice desk— not fancy, but sturdy and adequate. I ran my hands over the smooth wood and remembered how much more confident I felt behind it now than I had at first.

All at once, the Maelstrom of emotions that had been pent-up inside me could no longer be stayed. Although determined not to allow the tears to release, I cried anyway. I cried inside. Try as I might I could not extricate from my being the deep-rooted feelings of love for this simple little sanctuary—no, it wasn't the building, it was all it represented and all the people whose lives had been integrated into its structure.

God, it's so unfair. Why are you making me leave this place? Why me? I was happy here. You were blessing us and people were being saved. Now what? What's going to happen to this? What's going to happen to the Mennonites? What's going to happen to me? *They shall not understand now, but they shall later.*

Yes, God, I know, but how much later? Why couldn't you make them understand now so I wouldn't have to leave?

My fingers began to ache from clutching the front of the podium and I released them and picked up the hymn book that lay there. I was going to miss leading songs from that hymn book. I knew most of the page numbers by heart.

The sound of a car's engine interrupted the silence

and I froze. The last thing I wanted was for someone to find me here like this alone. The car came closer and I strained to look out the window. Pretty soon I saw the cloud of dust that signaled its approach. Lord, please let it go by. I can't talk to anyone right now. Not anyone. Besides, I'm not even supposed to be in here any more.

I held my breath and the car whizzed by in a dusty shroud. With a sigh of relief I relaxed. The clock on the back wall said it was time to go. Supper was waiting. I walked toward the door, down the aisle, and without a backward glance, stepped outside. That part of my life was behind me.

19

Tent Revival Preacher

The smell of orange blossoms saturated the air and it was a good day for setting up the tent. It was still hard for me to believe it was December, with all the warm sunshine and not even a remote possibility of snow by Christmas. Or by any other time, for that matter.

"Hey, Jack, bring me that sledgehammer out of the truck, will ya?" Amos yelled. His arms were loaded with dirty wooden stakes he was placing at intervals around the oval tent canvas that lay stretched out on the ground.

"Yeah, okay," Jack called back. "Let me know when you're ready to lift the center pole and I'll give you a hand."

"Aw, don't worry about that. I'll get it." Being raised on a farm had given Amos an edge when it came to brute muscular strength. He could lift that big heavy steel center pole by himself.

"Oh, when the battle's over, we shall wear a crown; yes, we shall wear a crown, Oh, we shall wear a crown—" Amos's voice rang out in boisterous song.

"Here you are, brother," Jack said, walking over to Amos with the sledgehammer. "Catch!" He raised the heavy tool in the air as if to throw it, then lowered his arms and began laughing at Amos's quick retake.

They made a good team. Jack Fries, a dark-eyed, handsome young man, hit it off right from the start with Amos who had married and brought Joy with him back to Florida. There was never a dull moment with Jack and Amos around. Their youthful vitality and slightly over-developed sense of humor generated excitement wherever they happened to be.

It had been almost a year since the Minnesota revival. Remembering the conditions of Grandpop Kaufman's gift of land for the Strawberry Lake parsonage, we'd arranged to pay $500 to the Missions Board of the North Central Mennonite District. We'd said "good-bye" to our loved ones and traveled down to Florida where we felt God had called us.

Linford Martin had become a part of the Gospel Crusade, Inc., the missions organization Henry Brunk had started in 1953. Linford was now holding evangelistic tent meetings under its auspices. He wrote and invited me to join him. Our first meeting was held in Ponchatoula, Louisiana, and it lasted for sixteen weeks. Although this type of ministry was totally new to me, I loved the freedom and excitement of it. As long as we were able to buy enough food for our families with the meager free-will offerings given, we were happy. I rejoiced at each individual's salvation or healing and I grasped at every opportunity to plumb the depths of this new Holy Spirit-led life.

However, after several months with Brother Martin, something began to really bother me about him. God seemed to give him a word of prophecy at the drop of a hat. He was always prophesying. Now, I was used to that, but as time went on and some of his directional prophecies didn't come to pass, I began to wonder.

One time he spoke prophetically that I should never shave my beard or cut my hair. Neither was I to wear white shirts—only solid-colored flannel ones. I was to be like Elijah.

It sounded strange, but I was obedient and followed his instructions for several weeks. My chin grew stubbly and itchy, but I wasn't feeling any holier as I looked into the mirror each morning. And Beulah was even unhappier with the situation than I.

"Gerald, I don't know about Linford," she said finally one night. "I just don't feel right about some of the things he's been saying."

"Yeah, I know what you mean," I answered. "I've been really checking out some of these prophecies and, Beulah, sometimes they don't even line up with the Scriptures. And if he says God told him something is going to happen and it doesn't, wouldn't that be a false prophecy?"

"I would think so," Beulah agreed. Her eyes dropped to the lower half of my face. "I wish you'd cut that thing off!"

I smiled. "What's the matter? Don't you think I'm better looking with a beard?" I grabbed her and began to nuzzle her face.

"Stop that now!" she squealed, trying to push away my prickly face and keep from laughing at the same time. "Stop it!"

I let go of her and started laughing. "Well, dear, if you really don't like it that much, maybe I'll think about shaving it off."

I had already made my decision about Linford anyway. My heart had been telling me for some time that he was going down the wrong track. Now I didn't want to follow any longer. I would take my chances at being disobedient. Besides, it would make Beulah happy.

When we got back to Sarasota, Florida, I shaved my beard and got my hair cut. Feeling my clean, normal self again, we started making plans to have a tent revival there. God used Henry Brunk to buy the necessary equipment—a tent, a large tractor-trailer in which to haul it, five hundred chairs, a Hammond organ, a new Chrysler New Yorker for our family, and a Spartan house trailer in which to live. We obtained the required permits and set up on the corner of Seventeenth Street and Tuttle Avenue.

We conducted tent revivals at that location for four months, beginning in December of 1955. Sarasota, known for its circus and beaches, was almost totally devoid of any kind of spiritual awakening in those days. We attracted a lot of people, including many Mennonites who wintered in Florida. I soon found out, however, that they were being discouraged from attending our meetings by Brother Brunner. They came, but they took a risk by doing so.

I met Jack Fries through one of these Mennonite couples. Frank and Ada Mae Stoltzfus had only one child, a lovely daughter who was planning to marry Jack. He was an aspiring baseball player who had embraced the Mennonite faith through the witness of the Stoltzfuses.

I performed their wedding ceremony, then asked Jack and Rhoda Ann to join our team. Jack's new bride expressed a keen interest in working with children, so we decided to start children's meetings in the afternoons. Jack became my song leader. He and Amos became the best of buddies and our three families became very close. We all lived in trailer homes parked around the tent.

When the lot across the street from our tent became available, the directors of Gospel Crusade felt impelled to purchase it. There was a regular group of believers who were coming out to the tent and many of them expressed a desire to form an organized body. Some were neighbors who lived in the nearby Leisure Lakes sub-division, and others were denominational church members who, after having seen the power of the Holy Spirit in action, were no longer content to go back to their stagnant churches.

Construction began with Henry Brunk overseeing and the doors to Leisure Lakes Tabernacle swung open on April 6, 1956. It was the beginning of a body of believers that exists today as a thriving charismatic church known as The Tabernacle.

Those early years were hard. Although I was considered the pastor, I could not deny God's calling as an evangelist and we continued to travel with the tent during the summer. We appointed elders and someone to pastor in my absence. It wasn't the best arrangement.

We began to receive invitations to bring our tent to other areas around the country. So we loaded the big new canvas tent into the trailer truck along with the organ and all the equipment and set off for Leeds, North Dakota. We made quite a caravan. Amos drove the big truck and Joy pulled their trailer behind the car. Jack and Rhoda Ann pulled their trailer behind their car, as did Beulah and I. Later on we acquired a dark blue Ford station wagon which we equipped with an elaborate sound system, including four horn-type loudspeakers on the roof. Before each revival, one of us would drive up and down the town streets with the Ford and play gospel music and announce our meetings. It definitely attracted attention.

Our first meeting in Leeds lasted for seven weeks and ended with the establishment of a community church there. Most of the people in that group were Lutherans who had been seeking a deeper experience with the Lord.

From Leeds we went to other small towns, most of them

on the fringes of large Mennonite communities. God was already fulfilling a part of His prophecy to me. *I'm going to take you to the outer edges of the Mennonite communities.* Word of our Minnesota revival had spread and it was from Mennonites who were seeking a deeper walk in the Spirit that we received invitations to come. Many people were led to Christ in those tent revivals. Many others received the gift of the Holy Spirit with speaking in tongues as well as physical healings.

One of the first healings God used me to bring about was that of a blind man. I'll never forget it. He was an older gentleman, the father of a local prominent physician. I was about midway through my sermon when I noticed this man rubbing his eyes. He seemed to be in some distress, so I stopped and asked, "Brother, are you all right?"

He stood up and all of a sudden began to shout. "I can see! I can see! Praise God, I can see!" His hands waved in the air as he jumped up and down. "Look at that flag there." He pointed to the big American flag we always pinned to the canvas behind the platform. "I can see all the colors and the stars and everything. It's beautiful!"

My own joy nearly matched his as I was reminded of the verse in Psalm 107:20, "He sent his word, and healed them." The power of the Word as it was being preached didn't even require a laying on of hands. This man's cataracts were dissolved as he sat in his seat and he was totally healed!

I grabbed the mike and told all the people there to stand up and praise the Lord. What a time of rejoicing we had. I knew God could heal because I'd seen it in the Osborn meetings years before and God had healed me. But to think that God would heal others through *my* ministry was a thrill of a different color. It was a humbling, yet wonderful, experience. Although not everyone I ever prayed for was instantly healed after that, there were many more miracles.

One of the most dramatic healings took place in our own family. And God used my wife to bring it about.

Our daughter, Joanne, was about five years old at the time and was being plagued by horrible nightmares. She'd wake up screaming in the night and run to our bedroom with tears streaming down her face. At times it would even happen in church when she would fall asleep on the floor or bench while I was preaching.

We prayed about it but Beulah was becoming increasingly concerned. The condition seemed to worsen.

Finally one night in the trailer after Joanne had had another of these nightmares, Beulah decided enough was enough. Grabbing the little girl's head between her hands she screamed, "Satan, in the name of Jesus come out of this body! Right now, I claim the blood of Jesus Christ and command you to let her alone! Get out of her and never come back! Thank you, Jesus, thank you, Jesus," she kept repeating. "I praise you for the blood you shed at Calvary."

Joanne stopped crying and a peace seemed to come over her. My wife looked up and noticed that three-year-old Philip was sitting on the couch, staring wide-eyed at her. She vaguely remembered hearing his footsteps scurrying the length of the trailer over to the couch while she was dealing with Joanne. The look on his face was unsettling, almost like someone or something other than Philip was staring through his eyes.

Joanne never had another nightmare like that. But a year later Philip started having the very same kind she had had. In a flash the scene of what had happened a year ago took form. By her not commanding Satan to go back to the pit where he belonged he had merely transferred his spirit to our other child, the closest most vulnerable being. Beulah knew exactly what to do and she did it. The children were both delivered from that moment on. Beulah became adept at fighting off the onslaughts of Satan. In later years when I had to travel and she had to stay home with the children who were in school, it seemed they were attacked by sickness or accidents only while I was gone and Beulah was alone. However, our reliance on God's Word was absolute and we never had a need for a family doctor. Beulah's faith got lots of exercise and the children developed a high respect for her prayers. They knew if they didn't feel well they only needed to tell mom who would promptly lay hands on them, pray and then tell them to get up and get ready for school. A sickness excuse from school was a rare document in our household.

Traveling on the road and living out of suitcases was no picnic, especially for Beulah. Our third child, Timothy Lee, was born on October 4, 1956, so she had her hands full. She became an expert at making a home out of the few square feet of the inside of a car. Gasoline stations doubled as laundromats, refreshment centers, recreation parks, and sometimes even motels, when we had to drive all night and needed a place to pull over for a couple hours' sleep. Restroom sinks were used to wash sticky little hands, brush teeth, and wash out diapers. If it was night time, the diapers were dried by catching the top edge in a rolled up car window and letting them flap outside the car until dry. Of course, when there are three little ones in the car there are never enough gas station stops, so there was the obligatory coffee can under the seat to be used in case of emergencies.

The biggest job was keeping everyone entertained. There were endless games of counting cars by color and looking for billboards. Beulah loved to sing so from an early age the children were surrounded with music. As they grew older they joined in and our whole family sang together for many years.

We never went without enough food to eat, but there were more than a few times when we had to divide the hamburgers, count out the French fries, and share the milk shakes. Sometimes an ice cream cone had to suffice.

One evening we were pulling the trailer on a long stretch of highway near Statesboro, Georgia. Knowing there was a state law which prohibited trailers on the road after dusk, we anxiously looked for the nearest spot we could hook up. The next town was further than we thought. Beulah was the first to notice the flashing red light behind the trailer.

"Gerry! There's a police car behind us. You better pull over!" she whispered to me, trying not to wake the children.

Looking to my right, I noticed several other trailers that had been pulled over. It was barely dark.

"Oh-oh. I was sure we could make it to the next town," I groaned. "We sure don't have money to throw away right now."

"You can say that again. We hardly have money for food, much less a fine," Beulah replied, settling back into her seat.

I eased the trailer onto the shoulder of the road and waited for the patrolman. Some small town nearby must support itself by setting up traps like this, I complained inwardly.

Noticing the glint of polished medals to my immediate left, I rolled down the window to look into the stern face of authority.

"Driver's license?" the voice connected to the uniform mumbled.

"Yes, sir," I answered, handing it to him.

The man glanced at my license, pulled out a pen, then started writing out a ticket.

"You do know it's against the law to pull your trailer after dark in the state of Georgia," he stated without looking up from his writing.

"Yes, sir, I did know that, and we were trying to make it to the next town. It just got darker a little faster than I thought it would."

"I'm going to have to give you a ticket," he replied. He wasn't going to give me any room to argue. "That'll be twenty-five dollars please."

"Twenty-five dollars?" I heard Beulah take a deep breath. "I'm sorry, sir, but I don't think we have that much money."

"Well, it's either that or go to jail, Mr. Derstine."

I knew I didn't have that much money in my pocket. "Beulah, do you have any cash in your purse?"

She was already digging through her handbag, scooping up bits of change from its depths. My stomach was beginning to churn.

"No, I really don't have much of anything either," she said, shaking her head. She stopped abruptly and looked at me. "The only other thing I can think of is the children's banks. There's some change in their piggy banks."

I grimaced. "I hate to do that—"

"But if we don't have a choice, we'll have to do it," Beulah answered.

"Give them to me and let's see how much there is."

She leaned over the back seat and fumbled around the sleeping children till she found the little plastic banks.

After they had been unplugged and all the coins were shaken out, there still wasn't enough. We added everything up and between us there was less than eighteen dollars.

By this time the policeman was getting fidgety. I think it started when he saw us shaking coins out of the piggy banks. I scooped up the money in my hands and held it out to him.

"I'm sorry, but this is absolutely all we have," I said, looking him squarely in the eye.

"Uh, that'll be enough," he muttered, pocketing the money and turning away. "You get that trailer parked the next town you come to now, ya hear?"

"Certainly, sir," I agreed, rolling up the window and then turning on the ignition. I was more than ready to turn in for the night.

20

Holy Rollers

The cross on the ceiling in our Minnesota home was a sign to mother and dad that the revival was not a work of the devil, but they still could not understand why we had changed our lives so drastically. They were sensitive to the whisperings in the community about all the crazy things that had happened and then when we announced that God had called us to Florida, their fears were revived.

At our urging they agreed to brave the highway and drive down to Florida to visit with us for a few weeks during our first tent revival in Sarasota. Mom never did like to travel. To this day traveling in anything that doesn't have its wheels planted firmly on the ground at all times is absolute madness to mom. But they were anxious to see what their son had gotten himself involved in. They parked the trailer they had borrowed next to ours, right beside the tent.

Beulah and I were overjoyed at the thought of mom and dad attending our evangelistic meetings. I knew that if they'd only come in and feel the presence of the Holy Spirit they would know it was real.

They did venture into the tent, and although they didn't exactly act enthusiastic or enter into clapping and raising of hands, at least they were there.

One night when mom and dad were in the service I spoke on the baptism of the Holy Spirit with the evidence of speaking in tongues. Throughout my sermon I kept glancing back at them, hoping to see some glimmer of interest. But their faces remained expressionless and detached. At the end of my message I gave an invitation for those who wanted to receive this baptism. To my disappointment, but not to my surprise, mom and dad's hands weren't among those that were lifted. Must not be the Lord's time yet, I thought, a little impatient with the Lord's timing. To make matters worse they got up and left the service.

A few minutes later as I was laying hands on the people who were up at the altar, I felt a tap on my shoulder. I opened my eyes and looked around. It was dad.

"Gerald, I think you better come over to the trailer right away," he said. His voice quivered and it looked as though something was terribly wrong.

I looked at him, puzzled. Before I could say anything, he continued, "Something's wrong with mom. Maybe she's got the baptism or something "

A thrill coursed through my being and I jumped up. "Praise the Lord!" I shouted. Spotting Beulah, I motioned for her to come at once.

"Beulah, come quickly over to the trailer with me. Mom's getting the baptism!"

"What?!"

"Just come!"

We ran out of the tent and opened the door to the little trailer Henry Brunk had let them use. Mom was sitting quietly at the table with an embarrassed grin on her face.

"Mom, what's going on?" I asked with eager curiosity.

She opened her mouth to reply, but instead of speaking in her normal way, a torrent of syllables in another language spilled from her lips. She clapped her hands over her mouth and put her head down on the table, jabbering away the whole time.

Beulah and I started laughing and praising God with all our might. It was unbelievable! Mom was speaking in tongues and she couldn't help herself.

She finally did get her mouth under control and with a big smile tried again to tell us what had happened. But it was to no avail. The same thing happened again.

I whirled around and grabbed dad by the shoulders. He looked bewildered.

"How did this happen, dad?" I asked.

"Well, I didn't know. I guess you saw us leave the meeting."

I nodded. "Yeah, you didn't look too happy."

"No. I mean, yes, that's right. Mom was having a hard time during the whole service and then when you started getting loud and shouting and clapping and everything, why she just wanted to leave. Well, as soon as we were out of the tent, she started to say something to me, and she just started jabberin' away like she is now."

It was too good to be true. I ran out of the trailer over to the tent and invited everyone to come over and see mom. She sat at the table, her face lit up. She couldn't believe it herself.

That whole night mom never was able to tell us exactly what happened or how she felt. Every time she felt like she'd gotten her vibrating jaws under control and would start to speak, it came out in unknown tongues.

The next day she very slowly and carefully told us her story. When she and dad left the meeting she had been more than a little upset. All the goings-on in the tent were too much for her and she made up her mind to talk to me about it the first chance she got. But as she turned to dad to verbalize her feelings she began to speak in tongues. God had given her the gift in spite of herself! It was a sovereign act of God, along the same lines of what happened to Saul of Tarsus in the Bible when God sovereignly arrested him on the road to Damascus.

Mom said she felt like her feet didn't touch the ground all that night. When she finally was able to go to bed, she had a vision of heaven in all its glory.

Mom was a different person after that. She had been touched by the fire.

"Gerald, you go on doing what you feel God has called you to do," she said. Dad received the infilling of the Holy Spirit several years later under the ministry of a Lutheran evangelist, Herb Mjorud—in a more conventional way. It has been a wonderful blessing to have mom and dad's full support since then.

For the next several summers we toured with the tent. From those experiences we received an accelerated course in Christian development and maturity. By trial and error we learned the ropes. We made mistakes. Many of them. It wasn't our lack of sincerity that brought them about. We just didn't always make the wisest decisions at the wisest times. Youthful impetuosity and zeal had more to do with it than anything. Years later we laughed at some of those episodes but at the time they were hardly laughing matters. In fact, one time I had to bail my two partners, Amos and Jack, out of jail.

It all started one night when we had the tent up in Sarasota. There was a good crowd there that night. Jack led the song service and I was moderating. We had invited Dr. Jonas Miller to be our guest speaker. Amos helped take up the offering, then collected the cups and slipped out of the tent. Finally I stood up and introduced Dr. Miller.

He was only a few minutes into his message when he was rudely interrupted by a loud, raspy voice that came from behind the last row of folding chairs.

"I'll fly away, O glory; I'll fly away—" the voice competed in an eerie, off-key tone with Dr. Miller's.

What in the world, I wondered. I strained my eyes against the spotlights to see.

". . . I'll fly away, O glory; I'll fly away—" the voice continued.

Oh-oh. It was Chester Duran. And he was in his usual state. Drunk as a cockroach that had just been sprayed with bug bomb. We'd gotten him saved once and even cast out the wine demon from him but he couldn't seem to kick the habit. His wife and children came to our meetings and often had come running to us when Chester was drunk. When in that state he was unpredictable and dangerous and once had even tried to burn their house down.

Dr. Miller concentrated on his words and raised his pitch just a little higher. Heads turned around to see what was going on, then tried to ignore the disturbance. But it wasn't easy. Chester either didn't know someone else had the floor at that moment or didn't care. He kept on with his one-man act.

He kept on, that is, until Amos and Jack couldn't sit still any longer. They tended to be a little less patient than I, and they felt, rightfully so, that it was their duty to keep order. I saw Amos stand up and then walk over to Chester, grab his arm and firmly steer him out the back flap of the tent. Jack was right behind them. I stifled a grin and relaxed as I settled back in my chair. They'd take care of things.

Did they ever take care of things. Jack told me later what happened. It seems when they got Chester out of the tent they decided their first order of business was to try and sober him up a little so he wouldn't be a nuisance. They certainly didn't want to send him home to his family. Amos came up with the idea to tie him up to a ladder to keep him out of trouble for a while. Amos always had an answer for everything. He was the kind of person that if there wasn't an obvious solution to something, he'd have no trouble creating one fast. He thrived on the excitement of emergencies. No wonder God gave him the name "Peter" during the revival.

Anyway, it was Amos who whipped off his leather belt. Before securing ol' Chester to the ladder, Amos gave him a couple of licks on the seat of his pants to shock him a little.

Needless to say, Chester didn't bother us for the rest of the service. But afterwards we still had the problem of what to do with him. He was still inebriated and we didn't want to send him home, but we couldn't leave him outside tied on a ladder either.

Everyone had gone home and Amos, Jack, and I sat around the red-hot smudge pot that was still burning. Winters in Florida could produce a few chilly nights and this was one of them. We'd borrowed an old smudge pot heater from an orange grove farmer to take the chill out of the drafty tent. You could hardly feel the heat if you were more than two feet away from it, but if you were any closer than that you'd scorch whatever side of you was facing the funnel-shaped tin pot. But it was better than nothing.

"How about if we let him come into the tent for the night," Jack suggested. "There are some old sacks we can let him sleep on."

"Yeah, I guess we could," I said. "But it will be pretty cold once we put out the smudge pot."

Amos had been leaning forward, his elbows resting on his knees. He was thinking. I could tell from the way his pale-blue eyes were staring, that he was hearing us but not really listening.

"Maybe we could leave the smudge pot burning then," Jack replied.

"Oh, that might be dangerous. He could tip the thing over and burn the whole place down," I said emphatically.

"You're right," Jack answered. "That wasn't a very good idea."

"Hey, I got it." Amos had the answer. "That's a good sturdy ladder he's on now. Why don't we bring it in and make a nice bed on it out of the gunny sacks we pack the chairs in. We can make it nice and comfortable, then put Chester on the bed and tie him back on the ladder. That way we can leave the pot burning. He can stay warm and sleep off the wine and we don't have to worry."

"H'm-m-m, I don't know—" I wasn't sure that was such a terrific idea. But it was the only thing we could think of at the time. Jack went for it and I was getting tired, so I gave in.

"Okay. Go ahead."

It was no sooner said than done. Chester was trussed

onto the ladder like an Indian papoose. We lifted up the ladder and set it close to the warmth of the heater. After the lights were turned out, all you could see were the flickering flames licking out of the tiny slits around the funnel-top of the pot. Chester was already snoozing. We stayed with him till about 3:00 AM, then went to bed. Very early the next morning we were awakened by someone yelling.

"Hey! Lemme outa here! Hey-y-y-y, help! Cut me loose!" By the time I got there, Amos had already untied Chester and given him several cups of hot coffee with buttered bread and let him go.

That evening, during the revival service, a sheriff's car pulled onto the tent grounds. He had a warrant for the arrest of Amos Stoltzfus and Jack Fries. "Assault and battery." We were dumbfounded. It seems Chester hadn't been quite as drunk as we thought and when he left our place and talked to some friends about what had happened they urged him to press charges. And he did!

I had to post a fifty-dollar bond to keep the guys out of jail. Then Beulah and I had to testify in court in their behalf. It was an embarrassing situation. We did learn that in the future we would have to deal with someone like Chester in a little different manner—or at least research our methods on sobering up someone. Either that or make sure they are drunk enough not to remember *anything* the next morning!

We didn't escape a little local persecution now and then. One night we had just ended the song service and I was starting to get into my message when a car with a loud muffler roared by, accompanied by some lusty "hallelujahs" yelled out the window. This happened several times.

Determined to use the incident to some good advantage, I stopped in mid-sentence and remarked to my congregation, "Hey, did you hear that? They're praising the Lord! That's the way I've been trying to get you to shout 'Hallelujah!' "

Later on that evening after the service had closed and Amos, Jack and I were shutting up the tent, we heard a car pull into the driveway. The sound of the muffler was familiar.

"Hey, you holy rollers in there! Come on out. We wanna see whatcha look like!" The sentence ended with a chorus of loud guffaws.

I grabbed Jack by the arm. "Come on, Jack. Let's go!"

He was game. "Yeah, Gerry. Let's show 'em what we look like."

We marched outside and walked up to their souped-up car that was stuffed with teen-age boys. They looked surprised to see us come out so quickly. But I think they were even more surprised at how we looked. We were only a few years older than themselves and we dressed like normal people. I think they expected us to be wearing long flowing robes with dangling crucifixes, pointing our fingers and scolding them for disrupting our services.

"Hello, boys!" I exclaimed with a broad smile. I walked right up to the window and looked in. "We heard you praising the Lord outside tonight and I want to thank you for that. I'm the preacher and I've been trying to get these people to say 'Hallelujah' like you guys were doing it."

There was dead silence except for little nervous squeaks from the car seats. They certainly seemed unprepared for this type of reaction.

Finally the driver of the car spoke up. His voice was barely audible.

"Uh, say, uh—when you havin' your next meeting?"

"Tomorrow night at seven-thirty," I answered quickly. "Why don't you guys come out and see first-hand what goes on inside the tent? It's a lot more exciting in there than out here!"

"You'd let us come in?" the boy asked, glancing up at me.

"Sure! We'd be glad to have you!"

The next evening they were there. Three of the boys and their girlfriends sat quietly in the back row. A couple of them gave their hearts to the Lord before the week was over. They came back many more times after that.

But the human elements weren't our only problems. We had the elements of nature to contend with too— wind and rain. When a rainstorm lasted too long, the ground would get dangerously soggy and if there was much wind we would have to station some of the stronger men in the congregation at each of the poles around the perimeter of the tent. Sometimes while I was preaching I would have to keep one eye on the poles in order to know just when we'd have to resort to physical manpower to hold them down. Usually I waited until I'd see several of them lift completely off the ground. Of course at the same time I'd have to reassure the people inside that they were absolutely safe and God would protect us. Those were definitely some of the more outstanding "faith-sharpening" times. However, one summer in 1957 when we were in Detroit Lakes, Minnesota, the inevitable happened.

It was during a typical northern Minnesota summer

thunderstorm. We were accustomed to the fury of these weather disturbances that often contained hail and high winds. Sizzling lightning bolts played a fast game of chase across the heavy black sky.

During this particular afternoon the weather conditions steadily deteriorated. We contemplated canceling the meeting for that night, but then decided against it. God would most certainly watch over us since we were worshiping and glorifying Him. He was in control of the storm anyway.

So we went ahead with the meeting that night. In spite of the weather, there was a good crowd there. Farmers couldn't work in their fields so when the weather was bad we had better crowds. The meeting progressed normally, although I kept a close eye on the heaving canvas and swaying poles and hard to preach a little louder over the roar of the pounding raindrops. When the service drew to a close I tacked a little prayer of thanks along with the benediction. It was a little earlier than usual but Beulah had started giving me "those" looks that only I could decipher and I thought it best to wind it down as soon as possible.

After the last person left, we closed the tent tightly and I invited Amos and his wife over to our place for a snack and some fellowship. The wind tore at our clothes as we tumbled into our trailer. We kicked off our shoes and were sitting around the living room alcove reviewing the events of the afternoon. The trailer rocked violently as a gust of wind caught it. All of a sudden we heard a gasp from Beulah who had been preparing some cold drinks.

"Oh, no! Gerald, look at the tent!" Her voice ended in a shriek as she leaned over the sink and stared out the window.

We all leaped up to look outside, just in time to see a huge parachute-type object settle slowly onto the ground and flatten out. It was our tent.

"Oh, my goodness—" I exclaimed. "Look at that!"

"Thank you, Jesus," Amos said slowly. "She went up like a balloon, didn't she—"

"I looked out the kitchen window and all I saw was the tent lifting right up off the ground," Beulah remarked, her face grimacing.

"Well, praise the Lord anyway," I said. I was trying desperately to keep my spirits from plunging to a fatal level. Looking out the window now, all we could see between the lightning flashes was the leveled canvas with little lumps and protrusions underneath and several poles standing at grotesque angles in the gloom.

"Think we oughta go out and look the thing over?" Amos asked. He was all ready for action.

"Yes, I guess we should after the rain subsides a little," I answered. Although I didn't say it out loud, I was dreading to go out and see our tent and all the equipment in ruins. Our sound equipment, the new Hammond organ, the chairs, not to mention the tent itself.

As soon as it was safe enough to go outside we went and inspected the damage. It was a mess. Water and mud covered everything. It was so hard to believe that one minute the tent had been standing taut and erect and the next minute it was limp and flattened. I wondered why God found it necessary to let this happen.

I was stepping gingerly over the wet tent, shining my flashlight around on the damage when I heard a shout from Jack.

"Hey, Gerald, look at this! Come here!"

I walked over to where he was standing next to a large object wrapped in canvas.

"Look at the organ! It must have rolled off the platform and somehow it rolled up in the canvas. You know, I don't even think it's damaged!"

Miraculously, the organ was still in perfect condition. It had fallen off the platform three feet to the ground and was wrapped up like it was ready for a moving van. That same organ is still in good working condition and has been used at our Minnesota retreat for many years.

Although we hadn't found any major damage to the equipment, I was still discouraged as I stamped the mud off my boots and reentered the trailer, dripping wet, in the wee hours of the morning. I told Beulah about the organ and she rejoiced with me over that, but she could tell I wasn't feeling too thrilled about the whole thing.

"You know, while you were out there tonight I was thinking," she said as she slipped out of her housecoat and slippers and sat on the edge of the bed. "Do you realize how short a time it was after the close of the service that the tent went up?"

I thought. It couldn't have been very long.

"Fifteen minutes. That's how long it was after the last person left. Now just think what a catastrophe it would have been if there had been people under that tent."

"You're right. We shouldn't think twice about the loss of *things*. What a tragedy if someone would have been hurt or killed—"

Beulah went on. "And do you realize how close our trailers are to the tent? Why we wouldn't have had a chance if these little cracker boxes would have gone up. Rhoda Ann told me they were on their knees praying their place would stay in one piece too.

"Yes, I know," I agreed. "We really should thank the Lord for sparing our lives. We asked God to protect us and that's what He did. Well, we've got a big day tomorrow—" Somehow things didn't seem nearly as bad as they had seemed a few minutes ago.

The next morning, upon closer inspection, we were relieved to find the destruction much less extensive than we had thought. There were a couple of king-size rips in the tent, but they could be mended. All together there was only about $100 worth of damage. Some of the local townspeople came out to help us clean up and before long the tent was set up again and we continued on with our ministry.

Our tent ministry in those years was concentrated mainly in Mennonite communities as we were invited by those who had heard about our revival and were hungry for the things of the Holy Spirit. However, in so doing we set ourselves up for persecution by other brethren who did not understand. It didn't happen frequently, but when it occurred it hurt deeply despite the fact we knew they just didn't understand at the time.

One time while I was preaching on the subject of praise in one of these communities, a Mennonite brother stood up in the congregation, pointed his finger at me and said, "You're a deceiver! You're taking Scripture out of context! The Bible says we're not supposed to show our emotions outwardly—only on the inside!"

I had enough boldness to tell him to sit down and stop disturbing the service. He complied and took his seat next to his embarrassed friends.

Another time while I was visiting with some friends, a Mennonite minister came by their home. I had my five-year-old daughter with me. If I'd known what was going to happen I certainly wouldn't have taken her.

The man was nice enough until we got to talking about the things of the Lord. He wasted no time in telling me, "I wouldn't go across the street to hear you preach!" Once started, his voice ran on, getting louder and louder. He called me a deceiver, said I was preaching heresy and was telling lies. All the while he kept shaking his finger in my face as his own face turned a glistening red.

Finally, when I could get a word in edgewise, I said, "But you would pray for me, wouldn't you?"

"Well, you sure need it!" he retorted. "You sure need it!"

I immediately knelt on my knees in front of him. "Will you pray for me now? I really do need all the prayer I can get."

My reaction discombobulated him for a minute, but it produced the results I had hoped for. He began to calm down and by the time I left, he had indeed offered a prayer for me and I in turn laid my hands on his head and asked the Lord's blessing on him.

As we walked out to the car, Joanne tugged on my sleeve. "Daddy, I'm afraid of that man," she said. For an instant I was tempted with a surge of anger towards the grown man who had acted so abominably in front of a child. With an effort, I smiled and patted her head, then reached down and squeezed her little hand reassuringly.

21

A Glimpse of Glory

I was perfectly happy as a tent-revival preacher. Not only was I a traveling evangelist, but I was pastor of the Leisure Lakes Tabernacle and had started several other churches. God had told me I would be going from "city to city" and although the places I'd visited were hardly what you'd call "cities," we were content with the hungry people who came and had their needs met.

Lately though, Beulah had begun to complain about living in a trailer after three years of raising our children in the eight feet by thirty-seven feet quarters.

"Gerald, it sure would be nice to have a real home again. The children are getting bigger and all this moving around all the time isn't good for them. It's not that I mind the traveling—it's good that we're all together. It's just that it would be nice to have a permanent home, one that we could spread out in a little more."

She was bringing this up quite a bit all of a sudden. I brushed it off at first, thinking she would get over it, that the Lord probably wanted us in the tent ministry for the rest of our lives.

For two winters we parked our trailer in Allebach's Trailer Park in Hatfield, Pennsylvania, while I established the Penn Ridge Full Gospel Church. The children had reached school age and we had to stay put at least during the school term. Although this was our home community, it somehow seemed foreign to us. We were treated like strangers among many of our own relatives and Mennonite friends. They liked us and, if we visited them, they seemed comfortable as long as the conversation stayed on the weather or farming or children. But they would stiffen the moment we broached a spiritual subject, and the walls would rise to form an impenetrable barrier. Beulah had a special burden for her six older brothers and sisters. Her mother was always warm and receptive although she was satisfied to stay the way she was. She had always been a devout Mennonite and regular churchgoer and was content to remain as such. My own two brothers had been born again and filled with the Holy Spirit through our witness and I was privileged to install both of them as elders in Full Gospel, charismatic churches. We claimed the verse in Acts 16:31 for the rest of Beulah's family.

It was at this time in our lives that God saw fit to put the machinery in motion that would further fulfill the prophecy He spoke to me. As I went through my mail one day in 1958 I came upon a letter from Demos Shakarian asking me to speak at the next international convention of the Full Gospel Business Men's Fellowship to be held at the Ambassador Hotel in Los Angeles.

I was flabbergasted. Me? A short, uneducated, timid Mennonite preacher? Speak to a crowd of fancy, well-learned men and women? I had been introduced to the FGBMFI the year before when they held a convention in Philadelphia. Someone had told us there were happy people there who told of experiences with the Holy Spirit similar to ours. When we attended some of the services we joyfully found it to be true and eagerly shared our experiences with several of the brethren there. We were thrilled to feel so accepted and loved among these people whom we had never met before in our lives. After the past few years of feeling so alone in our walk with the Lord it was like a tall, cool drink of ice water after a long, hot trek in a parched desert. But I felt like a country bumpkin next to some of these people who were so well-dressed, suave and confident. I couldn't imagine myself addressing a large group of people like that. Not only would I end up being embarrassed, but they would surely be embarrassed and uncomfortable for me once I started talking.

I looked down at the letter again, then looked at the envelope and the postmark: Los Angeles, California. Just that name evoked all kinds of images in my mind. Skyscrapers and movie stars. Rich people riding around in limousines. Beaches and bikinis. Smog. There was no doubt about it. I would most certainly feel out of place in a huge city like that.

"... We will take care of your travel expenses by plane and will provide your meals and lodging while you are here as our guest speaker . . ." the letter read. They were even offering to pay the expensive plane fare all the way from Philadelphia to Los Angeles. I couldn't believe it. Not just to hear me give my testimony. They were surely expecting a lot more than what I was capable of giving.

I folded the letter and slowly slid it back into the envelope. I had known all along what my answer would be. God had called me to preach about the things of His Spirit and wherever the door opened I had to walk in, even at the risk of making a complete fool of myself.

Besides, I still had plenty of time to prepare and I could even write out my whole message if need be.

When I showed the letter to Beulah she had the same mixture of bewilderment and excitement as I had.

"Do you think they're really serious?" she asked. "Do they know you've never spoken to a group like that before?"

"I don't know, Beulah," I said. "I don't know why they want me, but I feel the Lord is behind it somehow. I have to be faithful. What do you think? Do you think I should go?"

She hesitated while she smoothed the towel she was folding on the bed, then stopped and looked at me.

"If you feel the Lord wants you to go, then you should go. I'll have to stay with the children, but you go anyway. I'll be praying, you know that."

It all seemed like a dream. Even when Beulah took me to the airport and set the luggage down at the ticket counter, it didn't seem real. Then, as an extra-special blessing that just seemed to fit in with everything else, I met two speakers I'd been introduced to at the Philadelphia convention. One was Jim Brown, a Spirit-baptized Presbyterian, and the other was Earl Prickett, who had just been saved the year before. The three of us just happened to be taking the same flight, and with those two brothers in the Lord, it didn't take long for me to feel like one of them. They were just as normal and simple and down-to-earth as I was and they both were happier than anybody I'd ever seen.

When I unlocked the door to the hotel room that was reserved in my name and beheld the lavishness of it all, I almost felt guilty. All this would not have been necessary for me, I thought. And again I started to worry over what I could possibly say that would interest people that could stay in places like this.

Over the next couple of days before I was scheduled to speak, I wrote out reams of notes and Scripture references. I was going to be prepared. I had to do my best not to disappoint them.

"Dear Lord," I prayed. "Please give me the right words to say. I need your help. You know I can't do this alone. Give me your peace," I added, noting the butterflies that battled in my stomach whenever I thought about it.

Tuesday night, in the expansive room next to the Coconut Grove where Nat King Cole was performing, I mounted the podium and in front of 2,000 people began to talk about the things that had happened to us in Minnesota. As I started speaking, I felt myself reliving those experiences and the same anointing I had felt then once again descended on me. The butterflies were replaced with a bubbling well that sprang from within and flowed from my mouth to the sea of faces in front of me. It became imperative that these people grasp the urgent message of the impending worldwide revival God had promised us. They had to know how close it was and how real it was and how great it was going to be.

One hour and fifteen minutes later, I was interrupted by a powerful message in a spiritual language. I stopped speaking and bowed my head. The notes I had prepared lay untouched on the desk. I had totally forgotten about them.

Brother Jim Brown stepped up to the microphone beside me and gave a dynamic interpretation to the message in tongues, verifying all that I had spoken and reiterating the promise of revival. Even before he finished, a cloud of glory swept over the audience and thousands of people fell to their knees, some weeping openly and others praying loudly, their hands upstretched ed and faces turned upward. Gripped by conviction, others prostrated themselves on the floor as they cried out to God.

Unable to continue, I knelt in front of my chair while more prophetic words came forth, one after another, from people all over the audience. All I could do at that moment was offer all the thanks in my being, inadequate though it was, to God for what He had just done through me. I knew it had nothing to do with my own planning or ability and I was overwhelmed with what was taking place. People started coming up and asking me to pray for them. When the meeting finally drifted to a close, I had lost count of the scores of heads I had laid hands on and the hands I had pumped. Many of those hands had pressed paper into my palm. Not taking time to notice, I stuffed the paper into my coat pocket. Interspersed among the handshakes were many invitations to speak across the country.

In the wee hours of the morning I let myself into my hotel room, away at last from the babble of voices, and sat on the bed. I should have been dead tired, but my head was still whirling with the incredible exhilaration of the evening and all that had happened in such a few short hours. This had to be something like heaven.

Remembering the things I had slipped into my coat pocket, I reached in and pulled out wads of money and slips of paper with names and addresses. Ten-dollar bills, twenty-dollar bills, checks— I stopped and stared at one that had a five with two zeros behind it. $500! Someone I didn't even know had given me $500, no strings attached. It was too much. Certainly they must have made a mistake—put the decimal point in the wrong place or something. I probably shouldn't even try to cash it, I remonstrated.

My life was drastically changed from that day on. Meetings were set up for me all over the nation and I even received invitations to foreign countries. From a sawdust-floored tent I was elevated to elegant banquet rooms and hotel ballrooms. Churches of all denominations extended invitations for me to come and give my testimony—big churches in big cities and small churches in small towns. I shall always be grateful for the wonderful Full Gospel Business Men's Fellowship; these men have played such an important role in my life and in the lives of so many others like me.

Flying back to Philadelphia, I leaned back in the seat and closed my eyes. I thought of all I had to tell my wife. Beulah, you're not going to believe what's happening to that shy little stammering boy you married. I sure hope you're ready for all this. It's going to change your life too.

"Would you like a drink, sir?" a female voice was saying. I opened my eyes and looked up at the smartly dressed, young stewardess with her cart full of tiny liquor bottles.

"No, thank you," I smiled.

From city to city you shall go, and you shall minister to multitudes . . . teaching them about the things of my Spirit.

"But what about our people, the Mennonites?" The question carved a niche in my blissful reverie.

They shall not understand now, but they shall later.

Later. It had been several years now. I wished the "later" would come. I pictured the Ambassador Hotel ballroom filled with our people. If only they could feel that power we had felt. Just once.

The plane was roaring onto the runway and I leaned over to the window to search for Beulah's face among the crowd.

The $500 check was good, and our life was never the same. My testimony, along with pictures, was written up in the FGBMFI *Voice* magazine for three consecutive issues in the winter of 1959 and 1960. Calls came from all parts of the country, asking me to speak.

I felt obligated to keep the family together as much as possible, so I took them along if there was any way I could do so. The children learned how to conduct themselves in small-town church potluck dinners and posh hotel ballrooms. They slept on floors in people's homes and in car seats and hotel suites. In one small town where I conducted a series of meetings, our accommodations were in a former creamery building. We slept in the freezer, with makeshift beds on the floor.

In 1964 the Lord made it possible for me to take my family to the Orient for three months. We spent nine weeks in the country of Indonesia where we went from one end of Java to the other ministering in Evangelical and Mennonite churches. After our stomachs turned inside out and made the usual adjustment, we became quite fond of Chinese food. It was all we had to eat. In fact, I remember on the last night we spent in Djakarta, we took the children to the fancy new Hilton Hotel for a long-awaited treat—hamburgers, French fries and milk shakes. They gobbled the meal down in a jiffy—and ended up just as sick as when we'd first arrived and had to get used to Indonesian food.

We enrolled the children in correspondence schools during these times. Beulah supervised their teaching. It wasn't an ideal way to raise a family, but we felt the benefits were greater than they would have been if I would have had to leave them alone for long periods of time. And their experiences have proved invaluable to them as they've matured into adults. We're a close-knit family and it's enabled us to weather some pretty perilous straits. The children have gone through the same periods of rebellion other families experience, but from the time they were born, they were dedicated to God, and His principles were instilled in them. We haven't been perfect parents but I have the satisfaction of knowing our family has seen enough of the perfect one in us to copy Him and not us. That's the legacy I leave them.

During the late fifties, the church I had started in Sarasota, Florida, was having some serious problems and I felt obligated to return. After inducting one of the elders as pastor of the Penn Ridge church, we packed our things, hitched the trailer back onto the car and headed back to Florida. It turned out we were too late to prevent the church from splitting and we weathered some of the bitterest disillusionment we had experienced since the Minnesota revival. We were made painfully aware that even Spirit-filled Christians, in fact, even ministers, are still very human and susceptible to human weaknesses and tricks of Satan. My heart grieved for those in the congregation who were deeply hurt. I set about doing all I could to help heal the wounds of the few who had remained. Yet inside I was having a battle dealing with my own feelings of failure and disappointment.

During this time I had a strange thing happen to me. A dear family in the church had invited me over to their home for a meal. Beulah hadn't been able to come along so I was alone. We had known this family for many years and had become quite close to them. They were unusually spiritual people and there was a peace in that home that was instantly noticeable. During the meal, the conversation drifted to the church problem and I confessed my feelings of failure and helplessness. I needed this opportunity to be able to share the burden I was carrying with someone who I trusted and respected.

The main course was over and we were finishing our dessert when all of a sudden I was so totally overwhelmed with the burden of the church that I broke out in a loud sob. At the same time pictures began to pass in front of my eyes. I saw each of the five churches I had started, one by one, ending with the Sarasota church. Although they were well established, every one of them was having some sort of problem at this time. Then a scene that defies description unfolded before me. It resembled a cavernous corridor that stretched to infinity and it was brimming with a splendorous prismatic display of color that would make a rainbow drab by comparison. The depth and magnificence of it utterly humbled me and I felt simply unworthy. My friends who were sitting with me at the table seemed to dissolve into likenesses of Aquila and Priscilla, Paul's devoted friends in the Bible, and I felt sandwiched between the pages of the book of Acts.

Little by little, the picture faded and I became aware that I was still sitting at the table, crying in front of this family. Although I had no idea of the meaning of what I had just experienced, my burden had lifted and I felt incredibly light and free. There was no longer anything to worry about. God had everything under control and He would work everything out for His glory. I didn't have to carry the burden. A little embarrassed over my conduct, I thanked my hosts for the meal and went home.

Over the next couple of days I made an extensive search for an explanation of what had happened to me. On a plane en route back to Pennsylvania, I opened my Bible and tried to find something that would give me a clue, but there was nothing. I could still feel that awesome sensation of my glimpse of glory. There must be something in the Bible I could compare it to. But by the time the plane had landed I had still found nothing.

The next night as I was leading choruses in the Penn Ridge church I began to cry again. This was most unusual for me. I was unable to finish any of the choruses I started. By the end of the song service the whole congregation was crying. I didn't know what had come over us. I tried to read a few Scriptures and was intending to report to the people the results of my Florida visit. But I would just get a few words out and start to cry again. The whole service went on like this until a little Mennonite lady stood up in the back of the church.

"I must say something," she said. "I don't understand it, but all evening I've felt I had to say it."

"Go ahead, sister, say what's on your heart," I answered. I was surprised to see this lady talking out like this. She had never done it before.

"As I walked up the steps into the church tonight a Scripture came to me. It's Exodus 33:22, 23. I looked it up at once, but when I read it I couldn't really understand what it meant. But all through this meeting it's come back to me again and again. It must be for someone here other than me. In fact the Spirit seems to tell me it's for one person here."

"Would you read that Scripture out loud please?" I said.

"Surely," the lady answered. Picking up her Bible where it was lying open on the chair she read: " 'And it shall come to pass, while my glory passeth by, that I will put thee in a clift of the rock, and will cover thee with my hand while I pass by: And I will take away mine hand, and thou shalt see my back parts: but my face shall not be seen.' "

As soon as she had started reading that verse I was pierced with the realization that it was meant for me. Here was the explanation of what I had seen and experienced at my friends' home in Sarasota. Like Moses of old, I had seen the "back parts," or hinder parts, of God. A great sense of relief flooded my being and I knew without a doubt that this was it.

"Sister, that was for me," I said. "Thank you for being obedient to the Lord." I had not said anything of my experience before, but now that I knew what had happened, I shared it with the congregation.

After church that night I went home and read the entire thirty-third chapter of Exodus. It absolutely confirmed the experience I'd had. God did work out the problems in all of our churches. And He did it without my help and my worry.

In the fall of 1959 we felt led of God to return to Sarasota, Florida, for good. The wounded church there needed my leadership.

Along with the responsibilities of a pastorate came a parsonage, and Beulah was all too ready to give up the trailer home. God had finally given us a place to sink our roots into and it felt good. Only a handful of people remained with the tabernacle so we knew we had our work cut out for us. But it was a challenge and I had long ago learned to enjoy challenges.

22

Curls, Coverings, and Clothes

> In like manner also, that women adorn them-
> selves in modest apparel, with shamefacedness
> and sobriety; not with braided hair or gold, or
> pearls, or costly array: But (which becometh
> women professing godliness) with good works.
>
> (1 Tim. 2:9, 10)

Beulah was never one to fuss over her looks. Actually,
she never had to. Even as a Mennonite with a covering
on her head and no makeup, she had the fresh, sweet
coloring of spring flowers growing in a meadow. Hardly
ever devoid of expression, her face almost always
showed a degree of happiness. It still does. And it's not
because I'm such a terrific husband that she's happy so
much of the time, however much I'd like to take the
credit. She and the Lord have had a very special relationship from the beginning and many times I've marveled at
how quick God is to use her.

One of Beulah's physical attributes is her naturally
curly, light-brown hair. As a Mennonite she was required
to wear her hair up off her neck in a bun or knot of some
kind in order that the little prayer cap would cover it.
However, after we left the Mennonite church, I felt she
should let her hair loose and cover it with a special tulle

veiling that was longer. I had always read in the Bible that a woman's hair was her glory (1 Cor. 11:15), and personally felt it would be more proper for it to hang rather than be hidden in a knot. However, I still felt the head covering was mandatory.

Our church did not permit the women to curl their hair with rollers or permanents, so as she got older, Beulah learned to appreciate her naturally curly hair. As a youngster she didn't feel quite so blessed. Many tears were shed as her sisters spent hours combing through horrendous tangles in her almost-kinky mop.

But not everyone knew Beulah's hair curled naturally and the waviness did not go unnoticed.

During our early years in Sarasota, we used to have a guest speaker named Robert Barkley who came and ministered quite frequently. He was a prophet. Many times the Lord would show him things in the Spirit about people who would be sitting in the audience and he would call them out and relay to them what the Lord had said. He was a true prophet and the things he revealed were proved to be accurate. It was awesome at times how accurate he was.

One evening he was speaking in his distinctive, slow, quiet manner with his eyes closed most of the time, when he stopped and said: "There are two men here who have been arguing. They have been arguing over whether Beulah Derstine curls her hair or not. One has been saying she does, and the other has been saying it is naturally curly and she does not. . . ." He paused and then continued. "I see a terrible car wreck with one of these men in it. If these men leave here tonight without repenting of their sin, I fear for their lives."

He stopped and waited. The prophecy was so sudden

that most people hadn't even thought to bow their heads. Now several of them risked a furtive peek around the room. A weighty silence hung in the air. Then there was a shuffling and a man stood up.

"I am one of those men," he said softly.

Another man stood up across the aisle. "I am the other," he said.

With fear and trembling, they repented on the spot and asked forgiveness. As it turned out, they were Mennonite brethren from a local church, and thereafter we were accused of being spiritualists. After they went back and told the people in their church what had happened, the people were afraid to come to our meetings for fear someone would call them out of the congregation and expose their innermost thoughts or private sins. Since then, I have been relieved to realize God wouldn't do this to embarrass us, but only perhaps to fulfill His will in a given situation. He sees the end from the beginning and knows what is best for us. Sometimes I think He just wants to give us a little reminder to keep our lives in order at all times. Sometimes we so-called charismatic Christians get so caught up in our hallelujah-shouting, foot-stomping life styles that we lose the fear of God.

Another time when we were in a Mennonite community in Ohio with the tent, I had to separate two brethren who were arguing just outside the tent after the meeting. One of the men was telling the other how deceived I was and how dangerous I was while the other man defended me, saying I was only teaching the Bible and telling the truth as it should be told. Their argument had progressed to a heated point by the time I found out what was going on.

I stepped between them and put a hand on each of their shoulders. "Brethren, I paid rent for the use of these grounds and I want it to remain a peaceful place. If you must go on talking like this I must ask you to do it elsewhere."

The older of the men turned to me. "I've been preaching since before you were even born," he said hotly, then ignored me and went on with his debate.

I tried again. "If you've been preaching all those years, certainly you as a Mennonite believe in nonresistance, don't you?"

It didn't faze them.

"Look, why don't we pray?" I said persistently. With that, I proceeded to pray. Loudly. My hands still clutched each of their shoulders. I kept praying till they stopped arguing.

During those early years it was painful to be considered an outcast by ones whom I'd always been so close to. I guess it was hardest for me to accept the rejection of my minister colleagues; some of them were my relatives. I longed for the day when they would understand and experience the joyful new life we had discovered. Over and over again the Lord would remind me of His promise that *They will not understand now, but they shall later.* That promise was what sustained us. The "later" would come a lot farther down the road than I expected back then.

Our Mennonite tradition of nonconformity to the world (Rom. 12:2) in regards to clothing was deeply ingrained in us. Even after we were Spirit-filled and away from the denomination, we clung to the plain clothing for several years. Although we didn't impose our beliefs on anyone else any more, it was still hard not to judge at a glance whether a person was a Christian or not by the plainness of his apparel or the absence of jewelry and makeup or a tie. Many years of conditioning made it hard to break this habit.

The more we traveled in communities that were not Mennonite, however, the more conspicuous we began to feel. It finally got to the point where we felt we could become more effective by once again disregarding the plain clothes. I packed away my straight-cut suits and started wearing regular ones. Beulah was glad to be able to wear stylish store-bought dresses though she still left herself otherwise unadorned.

The last thing to go was Beulah's covering, or head veiling. Perhaps it was its significance as the last strong tie to our past, but for some reason I felt she should keep wearing it in accordance with 1 Corinthians 11. The Mennonite church had always considered it very important and I especially felt strongly about it. The style had changed somewhat through the years from when it resembled a Quaker bonnet centuries ago to the smaller, modified netting that fit close to the head today. It symbolized a woman's submission to her husband and the church—her "covering." The wearing of the covering was so implanted in me that I actually thought if Beulah did away with it a terrible tragedy would happen. We would be out of God's graces.

Beulah, however, did not share my convictions with the intensity I attached to them. She began to feel very uncomfortable about wearing it and she let me know it. It wasn't so bad when we were among Mennonites, but we were increasingly being used among other denominations and she felt others always wondered why she wore it. Actually, even when she was a member of the church she didn't particularly like the idea of the covering. In our church the women's coverings were required to have strings, or ribbons, attached to either side which had to be tied under the chin or tucked into the neck of the dress behind the shoulders. They could not dangle freely. Rules concerning strings varied from one district to another.

Before we were married, Beulah had gotten a visit from two deacons for not having strings on her covering. She had cut them off, declaring that since she didn't tie them like the old ladies, she had no use for them. Speaking in the Dutch language, the deacons solemnly exhorted her it was pride that made her resort to such an act of rebellion.

"We knew your father, and he wasn't proud. Your mother's not proud either, and we would hope you'd want to follow their example."

So Beulah sewed her strings back on—for a while anyway.

Now I stubbornly insisted she submit to me and keep the covering on. She was obedient but not without letting me know how she felt about it. Finally I got tired of feeling her heels dug in my back and decided I would leave the decision up to her.

"You do what you feel is right, Beulah," I told her, absolving myself from all responsibility in the matter. "I'm not going to insist you wear the veil any longer. You know how I've felt about it in the past, but now I'm going to leave it up to you."

Although I wasn't deliberately trying to lay guilt feelings on her, she knew me well enough to sense them. It didn't deter her though. With a sense of relief she neatly folded her head coverings and tucked them away.

It bothered me to see her without it at first. But the funny thing about it was that instead of making her less spiritual or more un-Christian and rebellious, my wife suddenly became much more loving and warm. She was even more affectionate and attentive than before and just as much a Christian. And there was no catastrophe or tragedy as a result of her decision.

As I studied the Word further, I found that the Holy Spirit is a woman's covering, just as He is the man's. Although she submits to her husband as the head of the family, Christ is her first head and He is all-sufficient as a covering. Facing myself honestly later on, I had to admit there was pride involved in my insisting on having my way. Whenever the question was raised, I would find myself thinking, what would others think? Or what if a Mennonite brother or sister sees her without the covering? It was as if she had to wear it just to prove we were still Christians.

Many times over I have marveled at the wisdom of God in giving me Beulah as my life's companion. She is indeed the heart of the family. I have always had to work at being affectionate and expressive at the right times, but not Beulah. She possesses that finely developed quality unique to women, especially mothers, which causes them to sense something long before it is actually seen or heard. It's that special something that translates a baby's cry or knows the instant you walk in the door that you've had a bad day at the office. Children grow to love and fear mothers for it. I am thankful to God for that extra little dose He gave my wife to make up for me. She's one of those old-fashioned women who feels totally fulfilled "just being a housewife." She respects and shares the calling of God on my life and is ready to pack a suitcase and go on a moment's notice. It's a rare combination.

There's another side to Beulah that only a select few see. It's the strong side of steel reserved for those who would attack her personal convictions, the truth, her husband, and her children. She will stand up to the best of them if the need arises. She has laid down her life for her family without hesitation and without resentment. I have been amazed many times by this side. It's effective. Sometimes it's risky—but it is always effective. Did someone say women are the "weaker vessel"?

My mother had a little harder time overcoming the clothing issue. When we returned to Minnesota after our first year in Florida we walked into the door of my parents' home.

"Gerald, I heard you're wearing brown shoes now," was mom's first remark after greeting us. She glanced down at the black shoes I had been careful to put on that morning.

I smiled as I looked into her eyes. "Yes, mom, that's true. I do have a pair of brown shoes now."

She pressed her lips together in a thin line and shook her head dolefully. "Oh, dear, I'm sorry to hear that, Gerald; I can't go along with you if you're going to start looking worldly." Her Pennsylvania Dutch voice was thick with disappointment.

"Look, mom," I said, putting my hand on her shoulder. "Don't follow me. Follow Jesus, okay?"

The next year when we returned for a visit, mom met me at the door again. After the usual greeting she said, "Gerald, tell me now, I've heard you've started wearing a tie. Is this true?"

Patting her on the shoulder again, I answered, "Yes, mom. But only a bow tie—just a little one."

"Oh, Gerald. I was afraid of that," she answered, shaking her head. "I had finally decided the shoes weren't so bad, but now this—wearing a tie. Oh, dear, you've just really gone too far. I can't follow you when you're going the way of the world like this."

"Mom, listen. Remember what I told you last year? Don't follow me. Follow Jesus!"

The year after that we came back for our annual visit. As we greeted each other I happened to glance down at mom's shoes. To my surprise and amusement, I noticed she had changed the style of her shoes. She had always worn the typically Mennonite black orthopedic-style shoe with strings, and now she had on a pair of more fashionable, loafer-type shoes.

Staring down at her feet, I couldn't resist the urge to step back and remark with a teasing grin, "Mom, I see you're growing!"

"Ach, get out!" she said, throwing her arms in the air. She turned quickly, but not before I glimpsed the smile and blush that flooded her cheeks.

23

Stirring Up the Ashes

"But, Lord, what about our people? What about the Mennonites?"

The question was never far from me. It was 1964 and nearly ten years had passed since God had promised a revival. Yes, we'd seen revival among thousands of people and many denominations. Things I had never dreamed of had taken place during those years with the result of many lives being transformed and renewed by God's Spirit. Yet my heart's cry was for my own people, the Mennonites. No matter how comfortable the settings I ministered in or how many people we met in countless cities around the country, I still felt like the same simple, tongue-tied preacher who really didn't know a whole lot apart from what the Holy Spirit did through me.

Many times I would think about Minnesota where it had all started. We had been back there several times and it seemed exactly the same as when we left. That was just it. It shouldn't have been the same. Something tremendous had taken place in that little community and there really wasn't anything to show for it. Somehow I felt responsible. There was some unfinished business that needed to be taken care of. Those people whose lives had been touched by that revival needed to have an opportunity to really understand what had happened.

There were only a few of us who had had the courage to step out—Mark Landes, Amos and Joy, Beulah and myself and a couple of others. The little Mennonite church had a new pastor who had rejected the whole thing and it dwindled down to almost nothing once again.

I began to pray about the matter. One day as I was sitting in my office in Sarasota, I was overwhelmed with such a burden for that community that I began to cry. "Jesus, what is it? What do you want me to do? Those people need to know more about your Holy Spirit and I feel responsible." I lay prostrate on the floor and cried out to the Lord. The burden weighed heavily on me.

As I lay there, the Lord seemed to give the answer I needed. We were to go back. A picture started to form in my mind. There were lots of summer resorts and fishing camps in that area. Although our home was twenty-five miles from town, the resorts around us were full of vacationers during the summer. Many people who lived in the cities had cottages on the lakes that they visited on weekends and holidays.

What was to stop us from forming a Christian camp? It could be a place where Christian families would go in the summer and relax; at the same time, they would be taught about the things of God. I had spoken in several church camps and had a vague idea of what it could be like. Then not only could the local people enjoy the benefits of coming to lively, spiritually uplifting meetings, but anyone else who wanted to take a vacation could make use of the facilities.

My mom and dad had bought our old house and the forty acres of property that went with it. I had no idea if they would want to sell, but it would be an ideal location.

When I told Beulah about what I felt the Lord was

showing me and she didn't think I was crazy, I decided to give dad and mom a call. This would be the final confirmation.

Their reaction was predictable. "But, Gerald, you wouldn't know how to go about a big project like that," was mom's reply when I told her what we had in mind. "You're not a businessman."

"Yes, mom, I know. But I feel that if we would take it step by step the Lord would help us to know how to do it. What I need to know before we do anything, though, is, would you sell us part of your land adjacent to the house, say, thirty acres?"

In the days that followed, mom and dad saw we were certain of what God had told us to do. It was then that mom told us of a strange, recurring dream she had. In her dream she saw many lights throughout the woods next to their house. And along with the lights there seemed to be many people. She had never really understood what the dream represented and it had puzzled her but when we talked of our plans she was suddenly reminded of it.

Mom and dad agreed to sell us the thirty acres which included two small cabins for the bargain-basement price of $1,000. That was our green light.

At almost the same time a piece of lakeside property with five cottages already on it went up for sale just a quarter-mile away. Feeling this five-acre tract on Strawberry Lake would fulfill the requirements of a full-service family camp, we negotiated on the price and secured the land.

So it was that ten years after God had visited us in such a phenomenal way, we were returning to the very same place where it had all happened but armed with another purpose in mind. We were really "babes in the woods" in

1954 when God had moved so sovereignly among us. Then we could not grasp the full import of what God had done. But now we knew. And because of the enlightenment God had given us, we felt responsible to share that knowledge with our friends who did not yet understand and any others who wanted to listen and learn.

After school ended for the summer, I took the family with me and we settled into one of the tiny, one-bedroom cabins on the thirty acres. Another carload of men who were volunteering their help followed us and moved into the other cabin next-door.

We almost felt like missionaries again. Water didn't come out of shiny kitchen faucets because there weren't any and indoor bathrooms were still almost as rare as they were ten years before. But the little wooden cubicle outside served us adequately and, despite the lack of conveniences, the cramped quarters and grueling hard work ahead of us, we enjoyed an excitement that goes hand-in-hand with being in the perfect will of God. This was home. This was where my life had really started. It was good to be back. I wondered if the others could sense the same electric in the air that I did.

The day after we arrived we armed ourselves with axes, chain saws, and brush-wackers and spotted out the land. Even though it smelled like summer it still felt like spring. But the sky was as flawless and sapphire-blue as ever. As we tramped through the woods a flash of color that I recognized as a deer snapped a twig and triggered a memory.

It was the one and only time I shot a deer. Those were the days we had to pick potatoes and fish at Jack Haw Lake to put food on the table. I had acquired a twelve-gauge shotgun and when hunting season opened, I had determined to try my stalking instincts on a deer. I had always thought I had a pretty good eye and a fairly steady hand.

"I'll have some nice fresh venison for supper tonight," I said casually to Beulah as I stepped out the door into the November snow. I didn't wait to hear her answer. Already I was entertaining visions of the aromatic meat piled high on one of Beulah's serving platters. The rack would look very nice on the living room wall. There were plenty of deer in the woods around our place. It would be a cinch to nail one.

I found my deer. In fact, in no time at all I had it lined up in the sight of my twelve-gauge with a "punkin-head" in the chamber and my finger on the trigger. He was a beauty, with a full rack of antlers on his head and every-thing. He stood perfectly still, a beautiful target poised like a statue in the ermine-white, powdery snow.

Shaking off a momentary twinge of regret at ending the life of something so exquisite, I squeezed the trigger. An instant later the buck dropped in his tracks.

Nothing to it, I congratulated myself. I was more of an expert marksman than I gave myself credit for.

Laying the gun down, and wriggling my fingers back into my gloves, I could barely contain my excitement. I picked up the gun and loped through the trees to where my prize lay.

But lo and behold, I no sooner reached the big buck than in one swift movement he leaped up and took off running. I couldn't believe my eyes. All I could do was stare in shock at the white of his tail bobbing away. By the time I collected my senses enough to jam another "punkin-head" in my gun and fire, he was gone.

When I got home I was relieved to see Beulah hadn't

waited for the venison for supper.

I gave up hunting after that. There were other more important things to do anyway and there were always neighbors kind enough to share their hunting stories—and their game—with us, although I could have done very well without the former.

Ah yes, this was home. I'd already begun feeling it miles away as we traveled the endless ribbons of road meandering between seas of brilliant sunflowers and glistening hay fields. You could travel for hours on those roads without seeing a single car or stoplight. Here and there a red stop sign broke the monotony and at night the only light was from the tall mercury yard lights of farms hidden in groves of trees. The only signs were ads for hybrid corn and occasional directions to resorts. If you weren't a regular visitor or permanent resident you could go for countless miles in the wrong direction. I didn't have to worry about that. Those roads were as familiar to me as the palm of my hand. I loved the uncluttered purity and simplicity that always coaxed me to relax and shuck off all pretenses.

Now as we stepped through the woods and took note of the layout of the land, I began to envision where we could put a tabernacle and motel rooms and cottages.

During that first summer we stepped off roads and began to carve out a clearing in the dense woods. None of us had been accustomed to that kind of intense manual labor and for days we nursed blistered hands, mosquito bites, and strained muscles where we didn't even know we had muscles. Every night before climbing into bed we had to closely inspect every inch of our bodies for wood ticks that burrowed under our skin. Beulah managed to put together three meals a day for the lot of us. I think she must have felt she was working in a lumber camp.

We finally cleared enough land to be able to hire a bulldozer that would cut into a hill and prepare a space that would be the basement of the tabernacle. It would be a rustic, split-level A-frame with the lower part serving as a dining hall.

In the summer of 1965 we held two weeks of camp meetings in the completed basement half of the building. It rained every day of those two weeks, but in spite of the dampness and mud, a warm candle was lit that would once again illuminate the lives of many people from the humble place that God had chosen to make His dramatic visitation years before. We didn't hear much from the local folks yet but had the feeling we were being watched.

The people who lived there ten years before were still there. It is the kind of place where the same summer people come every year and the few who have permanent homes there live, raise their families, and die in the same place. Changes come much more slowly and modern technology has less effect on these rural, simple-living people. Dirt roads give way to macadam, but cumbersome grain harvesters and hay balers don't go any faster. The few weeks of summer were and are a continual round of work, stopping only for the occasional neighbor who drives up the lane for coffee and chitchat about the weather and other neighbors.

The little Mennonite church I pastored still stands one-quarter mile down the road from the Christian Retreat. As of this writing it has not chosen to move into the deeper things of the Spirit. I grieve for it. And although people come from all over the world to enjoy our completed facility there during the summer months, it is only in recent years that some of those local people who had been in the revival with us and subsequently recanted are returning with open hearts. Grown and married now, many of their own children have come into the fullness of the Spirit and are on fire for God.

Amos and Joy are still sold out for the Lord and have three lovely grown children. Amos's hair is snow-white now, but he's still quick with a hearty "hallelujah" or "glory to God" and is still able to lead a rousing rendition of "Victory in Jesus." He's never lost his youthful countenance and zest for life and has carefully avoided the accounterments of the conventional nine-to-five way of living. We should all get as much out of life as that family has.

Beverly Carlton married a fine Christian man and they are missionaries to the Indians north of us near Red Lake, Ontario. Mark Landes became active in the ministry and has been a dear brother through the years, suffering the same rejection from the church that we did.

There are no words to describe the thrill Beulah and I have received over the reclamation of these dear people. There is a bond between us.

In that same year of 1965 I was inducted as president of the Gospel Crusade, Inc., taking over Henry Brunk's place. He had said years earlier that at the age of seventy he wished me to take over that position and he stuck with that decision. I was ready for it, carefully aware of the awesome responsibility it represented.

During the next couple of years help was volunteered and the A-frame tabernacle was constructed as well as motels, cottages, and utility buildings. Beulah, the children, and I spent our summers in one of the newly built cottages. However, an interesting thing happened. When we moved away from Minnesota for the first time, we sold all our new furniture to my Uncle Llewelyn who was planning to store it for his teen-aged daughter who would get married someday. It was hard for us to part with it as our parents had given the furniture to us as a wedding gift and we'd carted it all the way from Pennsylvania. However, with our future so uncertain, there was nothing else to do.

In the summer of 1967, I received a phone call.

"Gerry, this is Llewelyn." It was my uncle, whom we had seen only rarely since the days of the revival. When we did see him I got the feeling he felt I had gone overboard since then and he seemed uncomfortable in my presence. But when we were in the area, I always made an effort to visit him and his wife, remembering my uncle's part in my getting started in the ministry.

"Well, hello, Llewelyn. How are you?" I answered jovially.

"We're fine, I guess," he answered. "Say, Gerald, I heard about the camp you're getting started here, and there was something I wanted to ask you about. Remember the furniture I bought from you when you left in 1955?"

"Why, yes, I do. You bought it for your daughter."

"Yes. Mary got married out in Pennsylvania and she got her own furniture out there. When I got your things, I put them in a special shed and sealed it up tight so it was weatherproof and the stuff has been there ever since. Now I have no use for it, and when I heard you were back in these parts, I thought I'd call and see if you'd like to have it back. It's as good as when I got it from you and I'll sell it back to you at half the price I bought it from you. That is, if you want it."

I was incredulous. "You mean after all these years you

still have all our furniture?"

"Yes, and it's been stored and unused. You're welcome to have it back. We can't use it," my uncle answered. "We'd be glad to buy it back," I said. "We're just living in a small cottage during the summer here, but we'll put some of it in there and scatter the other things in some of the other cottages. Yes, I'll be delighted to buy it back."

Little did we know then that in another seven years we would be given the opportunity to buy back our original home, also, as well as the ten acres it set on next to the camp property. So it happened that after twenty years we were back in our first little home where God had visited us, with the exact same furnishings as good as new—almost as if time stood still at that spot. We were reimbursed for everything we'd given up with the extra benefit of a phenomenal interest rate—the retreat. We were far richer in many ways for having been obedient.

But do not fear, for I shall give you a greater ministry.

24

Florida Christian Retreat Is Born

The phone jangled on my desk in the Sarasota church office. Without looking up from the letters I was signing, I reached for the receiver.

"Hello!"

"Hello, Gerald?"

"Yes, Ezra. What can I do for you?" It was my head elder.

"Gerald, my wife and I are out here on a piece of property we thought you might be interested in seeing. We were looking for some land for ourselves, but as soon as we saw this piece we both felt it just might be the thing you're looking for."

"Really? Where is it? And how big a piece is it?" I asked.

"It's about ten miles east of Bradenton right on the Manatee River. There are 110 acres and it's beautiful. Seems to be good land too. High and dry. You'll have to see it, though," Ezra answered. His usually slow drawl was tinged with an excitement that was rare for Ezra.

"We'll be out as soon as we can get there," I said after getting directions from him.

I set the receiver back on its cradle and leaned back in my chair. I'd seldom heard him sound so enthused about something. He wasn't one who would waste a call on something that wasn't absolutely essential.

Although the subject of buying land for a Christian

retirement community had surfaced in several of our conversations lately, we hadn't really taken serious steps to initiate the project. In fact I'd been doing some serious praying about the matter although my main concern was not finding some land, but thinking of parceling out another segment of my time which was already so divided between evangelizing on the road and trying to be a pastor. I didn't enjoy the occasional grumblings about my being a part-time pastor. The worst of it was I knew they were probably true. On the other hand I also knew I had to be obedient to God's leading me to "the cities" and would continue to travel until He told me otherwise.

I loved my pastorate. Most of the people were my own converts and many were Mennonites who had been baptized in the Holy Spirit. I knew in my heart that they loved us too, despite the problems the church had experienced since it was founded. We had weathered the storms. Our children had grown up together and the fabric of their lives was closely interwoven with the church. The times I had tried to hand the reins of the pastorate over to someone else were times of anguish for me and the several times I had managed to do so didn't last long. Whenever a serious problem arose I was called back. Yet deep inside I knew I wasn't being fair to the people. They needed someone who could serve their needs on a full-time basis.

I walked the few steps over to the parsonage. It was late afternoon and we had to hurry if we were going to make it before dark.

"Come, Beulah. Get ready! We're going to look at some property," I called, slamming the door behind me.

Her heels clipped crisply over the freshly waxed

terrazzo floor. "What? What property, where?"

"Ezra and Margaret just called for us to come see some land in Bradenton that we might want for a retirement center. We have to hurry if we're going to make it before dark."

She was already looking for her purse. "Phil, you and Tim stick around. We'll be back before long," she said to the boys who were sitting at the table with their homework and transistor radio. Beulah had become a pro at getting ready on a moment's notice. She didn't want to be left out of anything and I was glad for it.

As we turned onto a narrow dirt road, overgrown with weeds, about 45 minutes later, I felt a tremor of excitement course through my body. I was surprised at how far out in the country it was. The last few miles before we'd turned into the lane we had passed nothing but large dairies surrounded by cattle herds and wide open meadows. We certainly had come off the beaten track.

I steered the car along the long, winding lane. Wide fields, overgrown with tall weeds and dotted with pines, spread out on either side of the road. A big clump of bamboo added to the tropical flavor. Further down the lane I noticed the most beautiful, huge Australian cedars I had ever seen. They were stately and of a velvety emerald color; they almost looked majestic. Interspersed among them were massive spreading oaks dripping with Spanish moss.

"Oh, Beulah," I exclaimed, shaking my head. "This is too nice. We'd never be able to afford the price they must be asking for this."

"H'm. From the way it looks, anyway. Well, we'll see," she answered. "If the Lord wants us to have it, we'll be able to afford it."

We passed what looked like a jungle of tall, gnarled vines on the left. Later we found out there were orange trees ensnarled in those vines—a little citrus grove.

We pulled up at the end of the lane to a big old gray lodge. It was a two-story frame house that had been built many years ago of timbers that had to be floated down the Manatee River which was directly behind the house and down a steep embankment. Other than the house, there were two little block buildings and a horse shed that was about to fall over from the decay. The buildings were all terribly run down and high weeds had taken over the place. As we walked around with Ezra and Margaret we found a cement-encased hole which used to be a swimming pool. It was cracked and deteriorating from lack of upkeep. A charming little goldfish pond was right next to the pool. There were healthy-looking, robust, bright orange goldfish paddling their way lazily through the seaweed.

"Ezra, this is perfect. You were right; it's tremendously beautiful. Just think if all these weeds were trimmed and this was made into a nice lawn—oh, they must want a bundle for this."

"No, that's the thing, Gerald," Ezra said. "Look at this." He read from a newspaper clipping. "This is what caught my eye. 'Priced for quick sale.' I've looked into it and it seems the bank is foreclosing on the lady who owns it—she has to sell. The realtor gave me a price of $165,000 for the seventy acres this side of the river. Another forty acres are across the river and that side's all undeveloped. That could also be a part of the deal. He said if the price didn't sound right to give him an offer."

"H'm-m-m, you know more about land than I do. The

price sounds way too much for us. Not that the property is not worth it. Think we should make them an offer?" I asked.

"Yes, I think we should," Margaret said. "But I think we should make an offer on the whole 110 acres. We'd probably get a better deal."

"It surely is beautiful out here," I breathed, taking in the gorgeous sunset that was spilling across the sky. "This would be the fulfillment of a dream." I was trying desperately to restrain myself from getting my hopes up. It was hard not to look around and form images in my mind of what could be. There was a low spot that could be dug out for a duck pond, with perhaps a building overlooking it with big glass windows. There would be plenty of room for homes for people who wanted to retire in a Christian community. Of course we would need a large tabernacle for meetings, and down the river we could make a nice area for services of baptism. We could have animals and tropical birds and boats and canoes. Above all, it would be away from the noise and pollution of the world—a peaceful place for Christians to come and be taught in the Word. It would be something like what we had in Minnesota, but much bigger and maybe even a year-round operation.

Yes, it was exactly what I was looking for. But was it what the Lord wanted for us? As the four of us stood on the grounds that night we agreed to make it a definite matter of prayer.

By the end of July, 1968, we had signed a contract for the 110 acres. Total cost—$105,000. An unbelievably low price for one of the choicest pieces of land in the county. We found out later that in recent years several people had tried to buy the same property at a much higher price but the owner was reluctant to let it go. God wanted us to have it. The bank agreed to give us $85,000 and we took out a mortgage on the remaining $20,000. That was just the beginning.

We decided we would try to have the land cleared enough so we could start having meetings on the grounds by that winter. It would take some doing.

The Ezra Laymans moved onto the grounds into the big gray lodge by the river and Beulah and I drove back and forth nearly every day from Sarasota. We began to find out just how much work was in store for us. Armed with scythes, axes, and heavy-duty work gloves we attacked the heavy brush and brambles that had taken over the place. The women set to work cleaning up the musty old house and when that was finished they came out and worked alongside us men. We killed two big rattlesnakes in the process of clearing the marshy thicket that lined the river and wore blisters upon blisters on our hands from pulling out vines from the roots in the orange grove. When we came upon a large slab of cement that used to be a tennis court, I decided we should use that as a base to pitch a tent for meetings There were long wide cracks in it with coarse weeds sticking up in single file. It didn't take long to clear it though and that first winter we rented a balloon tent that would seat about a hundred people and we set it over the tennis court.

Eager to inject the same enthusiasm I had into my congregation at the Sarasota Tabernacle, I convinced the church board we should close down our Sunday and Wednesday evening services and have everyone drive out to the retreat. Although not everyone was as thrilled about the idea as I was, most of the congregation did travel the long distance to the retreat for regular meetings. Of course, other people began coming out from the nearer town of Bradenton when they began to find out about the services.

The winter of 1968 proved to be full of surprises. Late in the fall, Beulah announced she was pregnant. Our oldest child, Joanne, had made plans to be married in the spring. Phil was in high school and our youngest was thirteen. Beulah was nearly forty. After recovering from the shock and turning a deaf ear to all the possible complications the doctors say a pregnancy at that age can present, we both set about reconciling ourselves to the situation. My wife, in true character, adapted herself and determined to make it a positive experience. Children have always been welcome to her. She requested one thing. She wanted to keep it a secret from the family and everyone else as long as possible. It was six months before anyone knew or suspected.

Stephen Paul was born on June 29, 1969, a robust, healthy little boy. I had gone on to Minnesota to open up our summer camp while Joanne and her new husband stayed with Beulah. She was scrubbing the kitchen floor only hours before she allowed herself to be rushed to the hospital to have the baby. Three days later she was packing boxes and moving all our belongings out of our house in Sarasota and into a little apartment on the Christian Retreat grounds. Two weeks after that she flew up to Minnesota with baby Stephen to join me. As we kissed "hello" over the little bundle between us at the airport there was room for nothing but joy and thankfulness for the blessing God had once again given to us in the form of a child.

While we were in Minnesota several other couples moved onto the retreat grounds in Florida and continued clearing the land and putting up the necessary buildings. We had left instructions and plans to build a home for us on the grounds and soon after that we called Henry Brunk and invited him to come and live on the grounds also. He agreed and construction was begun on a home for him right alongside ours. Despite the fact he was already in his seventies, Brother Brunk supervised the future construction of many of the buildings at Christian Retreat.

Henry has always been used to barking orders and putting to work anyone who is within earshot or walking distance. He loves to relate with a chuckle one day when construction on the campsite "washeteria" was underway. He had Margaret Layman and her sister, Louise, outside working with him when a truck full of cement pulled up. The black driver stepped out of the cab and yelled over to Henry.

"Where's your help?"

Henry waved an arm in the direction of Margaret and Louise.

"Here's my help," he said. The driver did a double take as he gave the middle-aged housewives the once over, then looked back at Henry to make sure he was serious.

Louise didn't flinch. "C'mon, Marg, let's go help 'em pour the cement."

"Guess I can help out a little too," the driver muttered, eyeing the women uneasily.

There were splotches of hardened cement over their dresses that night when the women went in to cook supper.

It was that way with everyone who came out to help that summer. People did jobs they wouldn't normally do and they did them willingly and happily. Even the children pitched in, mowing and clipping and picking up brush. It was a happy time.

After the first year we were able to move into our home on the retreat grounds. After much earnest prayer, the Lord sent in someone to take over my pastorate at the Sarasota Tabernacle and I was able to concentrate my energies at the retreat. We consulted with an architect and laid out the proposed plans for the total development of the place, then proceeded to get the proper zonings. We were advised to get all the zonings we would eventually need right from the beginning—five in all. This advice proved invaluable in the coming years since, when we began building extensively, it became increasingly hard to get approval from the county. We were made to comply with every letter of the law, plus, and as in everything that is done for the Lord, we naturally received a certain amount of opposition. In the final analysis all it did was give us a first-class retreat center that could stand the scrutiny of any inspector, comparable to the beauty of any secular resort anywhere in the country.

Sometimes we felt we were taking advanced training in the school of "living by faith." It always seemed to boil down to the monetary level. We never had the money to do something in advance. Yet we knew God had told us to begin. When we began putting up some of the big buildings it was all right in the beginning as we looked at the plans, signed contracts and gave the go-ahead to the contractors. The day of reckoning came, however, when we started getting those huge statements laid on our desk—especially the ones that needed to be paid immediately—the day they were brought in. There were a lot of Jericho marches around boxes of bills.

But now the place is complete. A one-of-its-kind, year-round conference center where retirees, young people and families live, and where thousands of people come to be strengthened in the faith. It is a living testimony that our God is a God of miracles.

God always has been, still is, and always will be true to His Word. He never let us down—sometimes He let us go till the very last minute, and sometimes beyond—but that's another story, for another book.

The Bible says, "Seek ye first the kingdom of God, and his righteousness; and all these things shall be added unto you" (Matt. 6:33). One of the biggest things that was "added unto" us was the fact that one by one each of our children chose to join Beulah and me in our continued ministry. First, there was Joanne and her husband, Gerald, who was well on his way in a medical career, then felt led of God to offer themselves full-time at Christian Retreat. Later on, after Phil had graduated with a degree in business administration from Oral Roberts University, he married and brought his wife, Jannette, to the retreat where they assist. Then Tim took a couple years of college, majoring in architecture before he married Bev, and decided to join the family and "be about his father's business." They have all dedicated their lives to the work of God and have not only helped in the administration of the retreat, but have been blessed with an abundance of musical talent.

To God be the glory. He always keeps His promises.

25

The Prophecy Fulfilled

The letter was in the stack of morning mail. My secretary, Ruth, had laid it carefully on top of the items she determined would need my personal attention.

The letterhead was what caught my eye. Souderton Mennonite Church, Souderton, Pennsylvania. I quickly unfolded the letter and read through the neatly typed short paragraphs.

". . . We would like to welcome you and your team to minister in the Souderton Mennonite congregation on Sunday morning. . . .

"You and your family would have about one hour of ministering time. You can feel free to plan the format of the hour in whatever way you discern the Spirit's leading. . . ."

I read it through again. And again. Was this possible? Was I dreaming? I couldn't believe it. They were asking me to speak. My own home church. The place where I'd grown up and married, where so many aunts and uncles and cousins, sisters and brothers, were members. The one place where for all these years I had longed to share the things of the Spirit, the blessings of the Lord. The place I knew would be the last one to invite me.

But here it was. Today. At this very moment I was holding a piece of paper that was an answer to more than twenty years of prayers.

Ruth walked in just then and read the smile on my face.

"You saw the letter?"

"Yes! Praise the Lord! I can hardly believe it! Do you know if Beulah's home?"

Without waiting for her answer, I reached for the phone to share the news with Beulah.

After writing my letter of acceptance in response to this exciting invitation, I began to get a little nervous. What would I say? Who would be there? What all had they heard about me and what would they be thinking? What should I wear?

Easter had already come and gone in the small community of Souderton, Pennsylvania. But the stiff biting wind that whipped around the corners of the old gray brick Mennonite church this Sunday morning in April made a last-ditch effort to stave off the spring sunshine that blazed stubbornly.

Souderton Mennonite Church. Twenty-two years had passed since I'd been welcome here, the place that had been a second home to me as a boy. It looked as severe and solemn as ever.

Now I was forty-eight and I was following the pastor onto the platform. Sitting down behind the pulpit, I had to pinch myself to make sure I wasn't dreaming. The place was startlingly familiar, and yet it wasn't. Instead of being without musical instruments, there was an organ playing now and I even noticed a piano on the other side of the sanctuary. I scanned the audience. The place was packed with Mennonites. My people. Only now there were neckties and bouffant hairdos and wedding rings. There were still some plain-suited older folks, but the younger generation had discarded the cape-dresses and straight-cut coats long ago. Many women even had their heads bare, without the traditional head covering that used to be so terribly important. Men and women were no longer separated by an aisle and families all sat together like in any other church. The Mennonite church had survived more change in the past twenty years than it had experienced in hundreds of previous years. They had been changes for the good, mainly. Healthy changes. The critical voices of those resistant to change were either left in the dust or stilled by the soothing tones of spiritual renewal.

My eyes moved to the front row where my own family sat. They took up a whole row. Joanne, Phil, Tim, all married with their spouses next to them and Stephen sitting quietly alongside Beulah. My heart beat a little faster at the beautiful picture they made. Look, people! See the fruit of my labor, the reward for suffering, the "all these things shall be added unto you" that follows "seek ye first the kingdom of God and his righteousness." Here's the proof that God honored the terribly formidable choice we made many years ago.

Funny, it didn't seem like twenty-eight years since Beulah and I had walked down that aisle all starry-eyed and dizzy-headed to say "I do." If we had known then what was before us— Beulah was smiling and staring without blinking at some undefined object and I could tell she was concentrating on keeping back the tears. Some members of her family were here this morning— relatives who for years had been cool and fearful of us were sitting in the rows behind her. Most of her family understood now because they had experienced the same touch of the Holy Spirit we had. In fact, it was Beulah, the baby of the family, whom they turned to for encouragement. It was the same with my own family. The love of Jesus had triumphed and things were vastly different. It showed in the firmness of a handshake, the readiness of a kiss on the cheek, and the invitations to share fellowship over a home-cooked dinner.

I looked at eight-year-old Stephen and grinned to myself. It was at this very place that my own dad had taken me out so many times behind the horse shed for a thrashing. And it was here where Peewee Derstine received his first call to be a missionary.

A lot had happened since then. During the past several years I was being asked more and more often to speak in Mennonite churches. The charismatic renewal of the past decade had cut a wide swath into the ranks of denominational churches throughout the country, sweeping the Mennonites along with it. One by one my colleagues in the ministry who had misunderstood and rejected me before were now coming back and asking forgiveness. Even Bishop Hunsicher and his wife had visited us in our Florida home and asked for reconciliation.

In 1975, in Landisville, Pennsylvania, at a Mennonite Renewal Conference, I had been informally welcomed back into the church and in 1977 it was officially recorded in one of our major publications. I was now being asked to speak at my alma mater, Eastern Mennonite College, on the things of the Holy Spirit.

However, I knew it would be some time before I would be accepted in many local fellowships. We Mennonites were a proud lot. There were still many of my people who had heard strange things about Gerald Derstine through the years and now to admit he may not have been the renegade they thought, would take a special dose of

Jesus Christ.

Now my heart was overwhelmed with love for these
people who I felt so much a part of. There was no bitter-
ness for the injustices of the past, only a profound love
and concern that they receive some of the blessings God
had given my family and me. Why I had been singled out
from among them for the path God had led me in was still
a mystery.

I recognized some of the faces that stared at me from
the pews. There was Bob, my teen-aged best friend, sitting
with his wife, Betty. He was now a successful real estate
broker who had also received the infilling of the Holy
Spirit. Uncles and aunts, some whom I hadn't seen in
ages, were now waiting to hear for themselves what this
maverick Mennonite had to say. I noted that there were
still the occasional elderly ones who came to Sunday
morning services to take a nap. At least they made the
effort to come.

The service was opened with a chorus. "I Will Sing of
the Mercies of the Lord Forever." How appropriate! The
mercies of the Lord were what had made this occasion a
reality. All the voices singing in a cappella, four-part
harmony sounded more beautiful than ever. Although
the organ had been playing before the service, the congregational singing was still led without accompaniment. I
had forgotten how nice it could sound. I added my tenor
voice along with the others.

"And now it is my privilege to introduce our guest
speaker this morning along with his family." The pastor
was about my age and was wearing a necktie. "He comes
to us from Christian Retreat in Florida and is on television now in this area as a teacher on the things of God's
Spirit. We are glad to have him back with us in his home

church. Brother Derstine—" I wondered if he had any idea of the full import of that statement. The place was silent, waiting, and I stood up.

I walked to the podium, smiled and greeted the people, then plunged in with something I knew had to be done.

"Beloved, I would like to begin by saying I am truly sorry for anything that I have done in the past that has caused any of you misunderstanding, bewilderment, or grief. I ask your forgiveness publicly and want you to know how humbly grateful I am to be invited to minister to you. I thank you for the prayers you've prayed in my behalf over the years, for I know many of you were genuinely concerned. Now I'm so happy to introduce you to my family—"

There. It was done. Now I was free to share my message with them. A message I had been waiting to share for so long. For the next thirty minutes I told them of the joys of the kingdom of God, how it was imperative to grow as a Christian and not just be a church member. "You are the answer to your neighbors' problems," I told them. "And only through the power of the Holy Spirit are you able to have the power to be a testimony to the world!" I poured out my heart to them. I so wanted them to understand.

I think they did understand. I knew it was all in God's perfect timetable and He would take it from there. Best of all, I felt accepted. I was back in the family.

The Boeing 727 lifted off the ground and circled over the towering dirty smokestacks and squatty brown buildings of Philadelphia as we headed back to Florida. The plane was packed with a mixture of people on their Easter vacations. My family was scattered throughout the plane.

In the private corridors of my mind I relived the events of the past couple of days. I reached over and found Beulah's hand. She looked at me and smiled, reading my thoughts.

"It really happened, didn't it? It wasn't a dream," she murmured sleepily.

"No, we weren't dreaming," I answered. "Remember how God told us twenty-two years ago: *The Mennonites will not understand now, but they shall later.* I think we've just seen the 'later'!"

The LOGOS JOURNAL for worldwide news— renewal trends—the best in records and book reviews. An inspirational magazine featuring columnists Jamie Buckingham, Harold Hill, Dennis Bennett, Iverna Tompkins, Gerald Derstine, Catherine Marshall, John and Elizabeth Sherrill and others.

For free information on obtaining a
book catalog, inspirational books
by famous writers, and the new
Logos Journal, write:

FREE
Logos Journal and Catalog
Box 191
Plainfield, NJ 07061

For authors and writers seeking information on publishing their own books:

Personal Book Publishing
201 Church Street
Plainfield, NJ 07060